JUGGLING

JUGGLING

Master the Skills of Juggling with Balls, Rings and Clubs

ILLUSTRATED BY
Jeremy Siddall

EDITED BY
Lydia Darbyshire

AN IMPRINT OF
RUNNING PRESS
PHILADELPHIA, PENNSYLVANIA

A QUINTET BOOK

Canadian representatives:
General Publishing Co., Ltd.
30 Lesmill Road, Don Mills
Ontario M3B 2T6

9 8 7 6 5 4 3 2 1
Digit on the right indicates the number of this printing

Library of Congress
Cataloging-in-Publication Number
93–70589

ISBN 1–56138–224–8

This book was designed and produced by
Quintet Publishing Limited
6 Blundell Street
London N7 9BH

Creative Director: Richard Dewing
Designer: James Lawrence
Project Editor: Stefanie Foster
Photographer: Martin Norris

Quintet Publishing would like to extend very special thanks to Peter Owen for his considerable help in preparing the manuscript and illustrations for this book.

Typeset in Great Britain by
Central Southern Typesetters, Eastbourne
Manufactured in Singapore by Eray Scan Pte Ltd.
Printed in Singapore by Star Standard Industries Pte Ltd.

Published by Courage Books, an imprint of
Running Press Book Publishers
125 South Twenty-second Street
Philadelphia, Pennsylvania 19103–4399

Quintet Publishing would like to thank *More Balls Than Most* for generously providing equipment for photography and for their help in preparing text and illustrations.

CONTENTS

INTRODUCTION

Most of us have admired the skills of the jugglers we have seen in circuses or on television. We have probably seen and appreciated street entertainers who include juggling tricks in their routines. However, memories of dropped catches and butter-fingered moments at school may have deterred us from taking up juggling ourselves, and even though we may have been tempted by a bowl of apples or tangerines or even by some small stones from the garden, few of us have thought seriously about taking up juggling as a hobby.

Yet juggling is a wonderful form of exercise, which offers tremendous benefits in terms of health but which is wholly uncompetitive. You can juggle by yourself at home or you can juggle with friends. You can confine yourself to routines with three balls or you can extend your range to rings and clubs or to five or seven balls. Juggling can be as simple or as complex as you want to make it.

The current upsurge of interest in juggling has meant that clubs and conventions are now organized in many towns and cities, and you should be able to see jugglers performing a range of routines and patterns. It is also easier now to buy the special balls, clubs, and rings that you will need if you get hooked on juggling and want to perform in public.

Public performances are, of course, far from your thoughts as you begin, but juggling tricks or moves are generally designed to amuse or amaze onlookers, and as you acquire new skills and gain confidence, you may surprise yourself and find yourself entertaining a few friends or a children's party.

Juggling and Health

The continuous movement required by juggling is good for the whole body, and even if you took up juggling for fun, you will find that it has a beneficial effect on your general health.

At first, you may find that your back aches a little. You will probably spend a good deal of time bending down to pick up the props that you have dropped, and you might find it helpful to practice over a bed so that you don't have to bend down too far. However, as your expertise improves, you will be able to move around as you juggle, and some people even juggle while they jog!

Juggling may be defined as an act of dexterity or of manipulation, and the verb to juggle can mean to toss, hold, balance, handle, or otherwise manipulate objects in a skillful manner in a show of manual dexterity. The whole activity does require a degree of concentration, and this in itself can be beneficial. You will find that the effort involved in concentrating on your props and on the patterns you are learning will improve your general levels of concentration when you come to apply them to other activities.

Enhancing your hand-eye coordination is one of the most obvious benefits accruing from juggling, but you will also find that it improves your accuracy in throwing and catching; your reflexes; and your timing, rhythm, and balance. You will also find that the activity of juggling is relaxing. It can make the ideal break from the pressures of home or office, and you will return to your work refreshed and reinvigorated.

If you work with your hands, you will find that learning to juggle will improve your dexterity. Because it requires accuracy and patience, juggling is the ideal pastime for anyone who uses his hands, whether it is for delicate work such as dentistry or a more robust occupation such as assembly-line work.

Juggling can also improve your self-confidence, poise, and stage presence. As your skills improve and the number of balls that you successfully catch and throw steadily increases, you will feel better and more assured, and your more positive view of yourself will be reflected in your everyday life.

Although for many people juggling is, and always will be, a solitary pastime, it can also be a very sociable activity. Many people join clubs so that they can juggle with a partner. When you are sufficiently skilled, you may want to teach others how to juggle – and you will be surprised at how much you will learn through the experience of teaching others.

But whatever reasons you have for taking up juggling, remember that it is fun. There is always a new challenge to be met and a new sense of achievement to be won – and you will be enjoying yourself at the same time.

EQUIPMENT

Most people think of balls, clubs, or hoops when they hear the word juggling. In fact, beanbags, which can be spherical or cuboid, are ideal for all movements except bouncing patterns, especially when you are learning. Throughout this book, however, unless movements are specifically designed to be carried out with a particular type of apparatus, the word ball is used. (See also Chapter 1)

GETTING STARTED

- This book is organized in a logical order. You should work through it from beginning to end rather than dipping in and out. Each movement builds on the skills learned in executing the previous one.
- Juggling can be a sociable activity – whenever you can, juggle with a friend. You will find it a great help to have someone else watch your movements and offer advice and criticism – and, of course, many of the movements are most effectively done with a partner.
- Concentrate on what you are doing. Think about the rhythm you are trying to establish and the order in which you are throwing your props. One of the benefits to be derived from juggling is that it requires a whole hearted commitment – you can't worry about your work while you are juggling.
- Juggling movements are learned by breaking down each pattern into its smallest steps and by building them up into a whole. This is true of all the patterns in this book, and when you come to learn other movements you should follow the same procedure. If you always do this, no juggling movement or pattern will be too difficult for you to learn.
- Learn to begin and end each pattern and routine neatly and cleanly. Don't just keep going until you drop something. Decide how many throws and catches you are going to do, and then stop.
- Don't despair if you cannot settle into a rhythm and have difficulty throwing the balls to a uniform height every time. Relax and try again. You will acquire the skills with patience.
- Vary the speed and height of your juggling. A movement can look very different when it is done slowly and with high throws from when it is done quickly and with little height.

WHICH HAND?

Because people are naturally right- or left-handed, you will automatically find yourself using one hand more than the other. Throughout this book, the words *dominant* and *subordinate* are used instead of right and left hands. If you are right-handed, your right hand will be dominant and your left hand will be subordinate; if you are left-handed the opposite will be the case. One of the great benefits of juggling is that it encourages a degree of ambidexterity, and your weaker hand will gradually become stronger. Nevertheless, it is always a good idea to practice all the movements until you are equally proficient at starting and finishing with either hand.

BASIC THREE-BALL JUGGLING

Perhaps the best objects for beginners to use are beanbags, which do not bounce and are easier to handle than balls. They are flexible and sufficiently heavy to fall easily into your hand. As the name suggests, these were originally bags made of strong cloth, such as calico or gabardine, and filled with well-dried beans, peas, or lentils. You can, of course, make your own, and if you do, you should aim to make them with a diameter of 3–4 inches so that they fit snugly into the palm of your hand. However, you will find that a vast range of beanbags is available commercially. They are made with from four to eight segments and are produced in a variety of colors – even luminous pink and green – and different materials, including leather- and suede-look finishes. You can even buy presentation boxes – the perfect gift!

As you gain confidence and experience, you might want to use larger balls. If you ever perform in public, you will certainly need to use balls that will be clearly visible to your audience, and "stage balls," as they are known, are widely available in a range of colors, sizes, and weights. You can even buy transparent balls. Extra-bouncy balls are also available for stage work. Some jugglers like to work with the rubber balls used for playing lacrosse, while others prefer to use the silicon balls that are specially made for jugglers, although these are rather expensive.

The Basic Patterns

Three basic patterns from which hundreds of variations can be developed are the cascade, the shower, and columns. As you become more proficient, you will be able to devise your own variations – the possibilities are virtually limitless – but it is important that you master these three basic patterns thoroughly.

Learn juggling patterns step by step. The keys to success are consistency and repetition. You can measure your improvement by simply counting the number of consecutive throws you make, and it is a good idea to keep a simple diary to record the catches you make in different movements. Monitoring your progress in this way and seeing the improvements you make will encourage you to persevere.

Remember that the throw is the most important part of any movement. If the throw is accurate, the catch should be automatic. However, beginners sometimes have problems with catching, and they find that the ball smacks into their hands. The ideal is for the hand to move up slightly to catch the ball and draw it down gently. You might find it helpful to warm up, gently throwing a ball to and fro for a while before you begin to juggle.

When you are beginning to juggle, you must resist the temptation to throw the objects slightly forward. It is essential that the balls, rings, or whatever you use are thrown vertically. If you have a tendency to throw forward, you will find that you will quickly lose your rhythm, because you will have to move your arms to reach the objects – and you will soon have objects cascading all around you. One way of overcoming the tendency to throw forward is to stand no more than your arm's length in front of a wall while you practice.

TIP

It is essential when you are juggling to think in two dimensions only – height and width, not depth. Try to visualize an imaginary frame in front of you, and throw to equal heights on each side as if you were trying to hit the top corners. Don't break out of your frame by throwing forward or backward.

JUGGLING TAKES PLACE IN TWO DIMENSIONS – HEIGHT AND WIDTH – NOT IN DEPTH

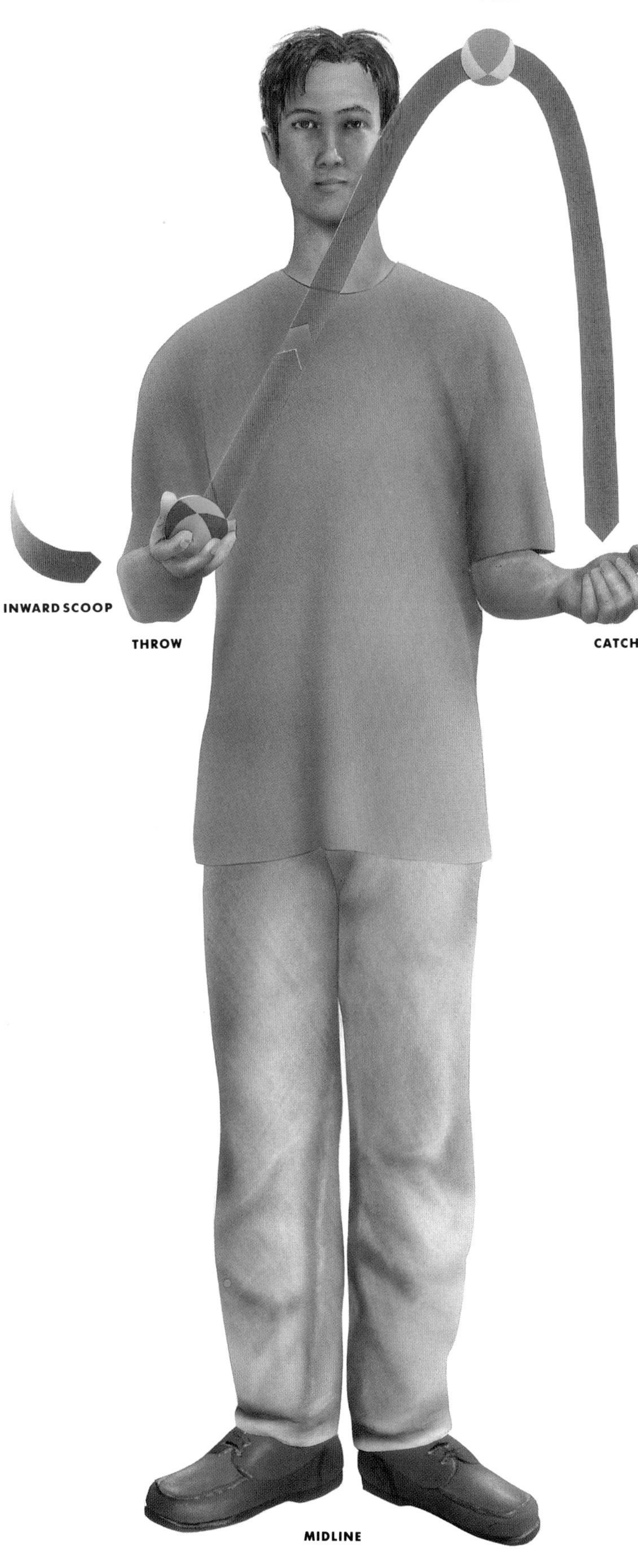

Standing with heels together and toes turned outward can help in making you juggle within two dimensions. It may be difficult at first, but is well worth the effort, and also looks good.

THE CASCADE

ONE BALL

Begin with one ball. Your hands should make an inward "scooping" movement as you throw it from hand to hand, and you should aim for a figure-eight movement.

TIP

When you are learning, imagine that you are juggling in a telephone booth. The ceiling is only about 12 inches above your head, and the fragile glass wall is just a short distance in front of you. Keep your balls within this imaginary framework.

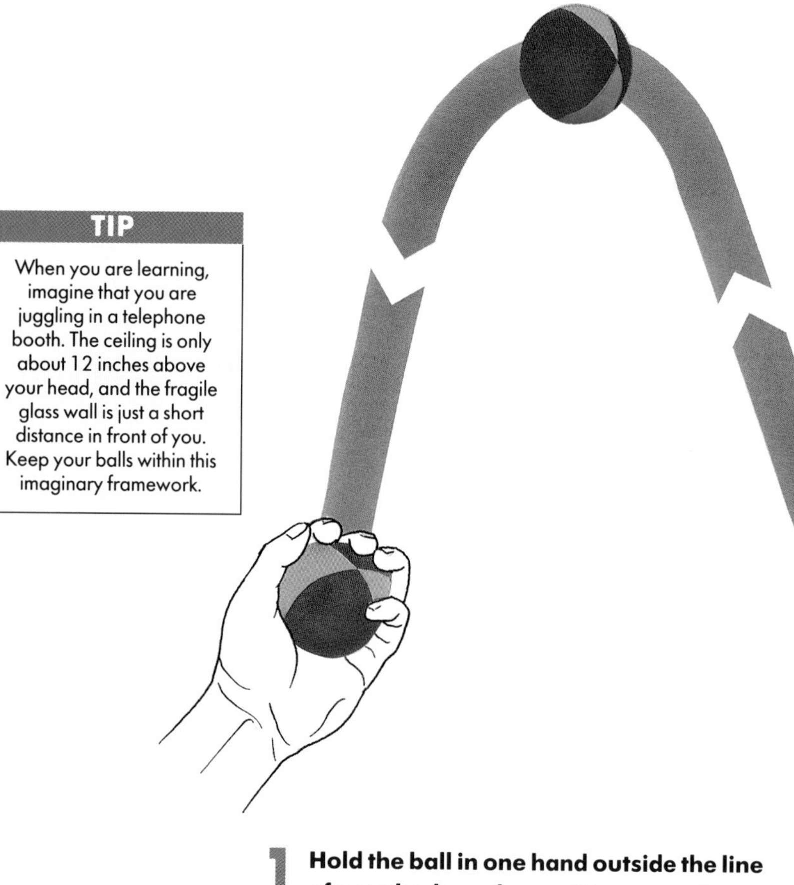

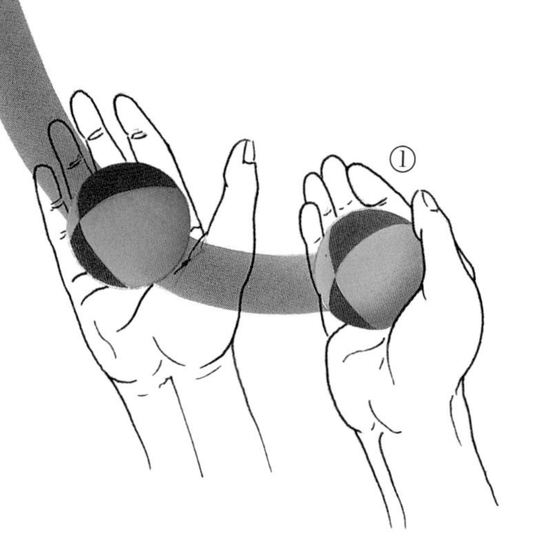

1 Hold the ball in one hand outside the line of your body and carry it in a scooping motion toward the midline, releasing it as it nears the midpoint.

The peak of the trajectory should be 12–18 inches above shoulder height at each side.

REMEMBER

- **Keep the movement of the ball within one plane, resisting the temptation to throw it forward or backward.**
- **Keep the palms of your hands upward to both throw and catch.**
- **Don't watch the path of the ball, only the peak of each throw.**

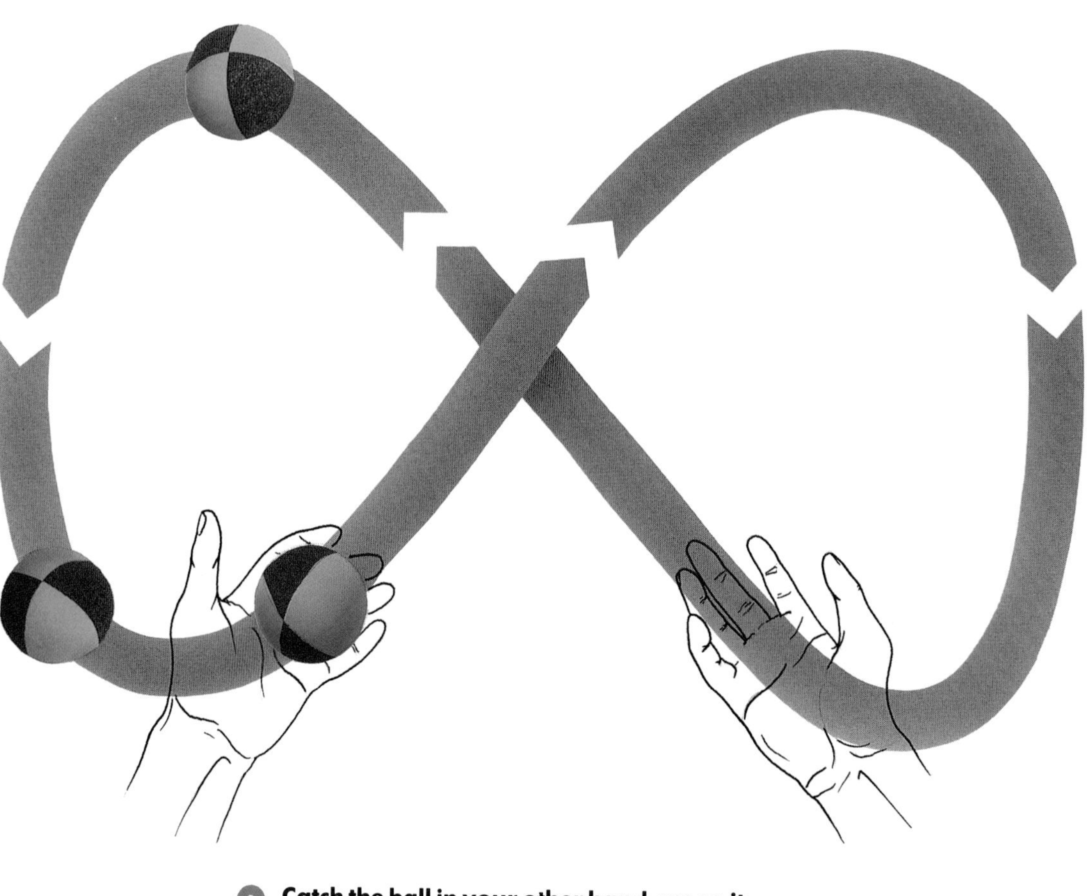

2 Catch the ball in your other hand, scoop it under toward the midline of your body in a U-shape, and release it again.

TWO BALLS

When you can comfortably and rhythmically throw one ball from hand to hand, move on to two balls.

REMEMBER

- **Throw both balls to the same height – imagine the frame in front of you and aim both balls into the top corners.**
- **To help build up a rhythm, say "Throw-throw-catch-catch" as you perform each action.**

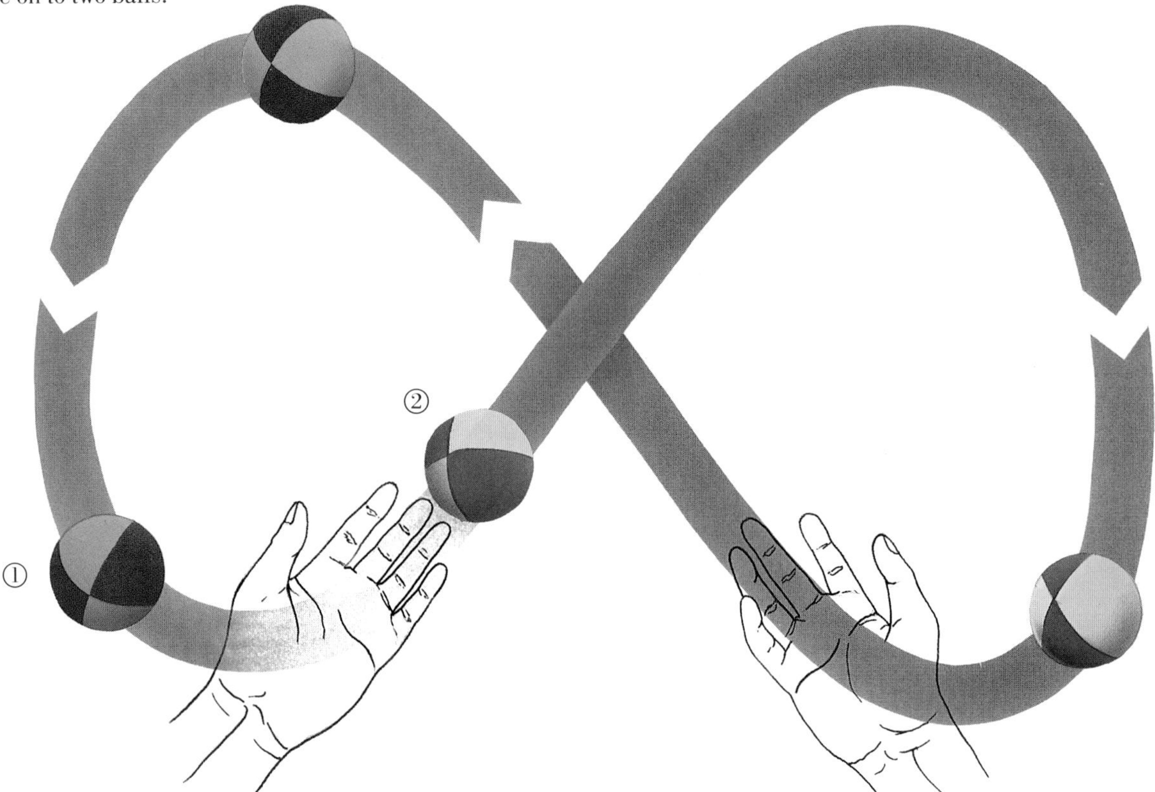

TIP

As you practice, you may find yourself repeating the same error time and again. If this happens, stop the moment you make the mistake and try to think through the movement, step by step, working out exactly what you are doing and where things are going wrong.

3 Hold a ball in each hand and begin with your dominant hand, throwing the ball as before. When the ball reaches the high point of its trajectory, throw the second ball with your subordinate hand so that the paths of the balls cross in front of your chest.

Catch the first ball, catch the second ball, and repeat.

A common error, especially among people who have learned to juggle with two balls, is to pass the second ball to the dominant hand rather than throwing it. An excellent way of breaking this habit is to begin the movement with your subordinate hand. Because your dominant hand already throws well, you may not be tempted to pass the second ball.

Another mistake frequently made is to throw both balls at the same time. Always wait until the first ball reaches the height of its trajectory before releasing the second ball.

Because the balls thrown by each hand will have different trajectories, they should not meet or kiss in the middle. However, if you find that the balls keep kissing in the air, it could be because you have not thrown them correctly. Practice with one ball again, throwing it from hand to hand to establish the correct trajectory, before working with two.

Finally, do not reach up to try to catch the balls at eye level, which is often done by people who are not used to throwing and catching. Allow the balls to fall so that you catch them at a point between your waist and chest.

THREE BALLS

In order to juggle with three balls, you will start and finish with one ball in one hand and two balls in the other hand. Before you begin this movement, practice holding three balls. Take a ball in each hand and hold the third ball between the thumb, forefinger, and middle finger of your dominant hand. Now, throw this third ball from hand to hand, holding the other balls in your hands while you do so. When you feel comfortable holding, throwing, and catching with an extra ball in your hands, you are ready to learn the three-ball cascade.

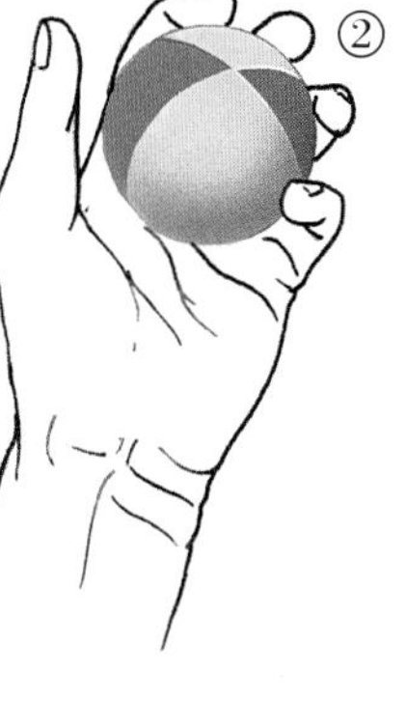

4 Hold two balls in your dominant hand and one in your subordinate hand.

TIP

A useful way of overcoming errors is always to catch the props in the same order you throw them, and this is why it is helpful to use different colored balls or beanbags. If you throw a red one first, catch it first.

TIP

If you find this step difficult, only practice throwing and just let your balls or beanbags fall to the floor. Say "Throw-throw-drop-drop" or "Throw-throw-plop-plop" to establish your rhythm, and then, when you feel comfortable with the throws, try catching your props before they hit the floor.

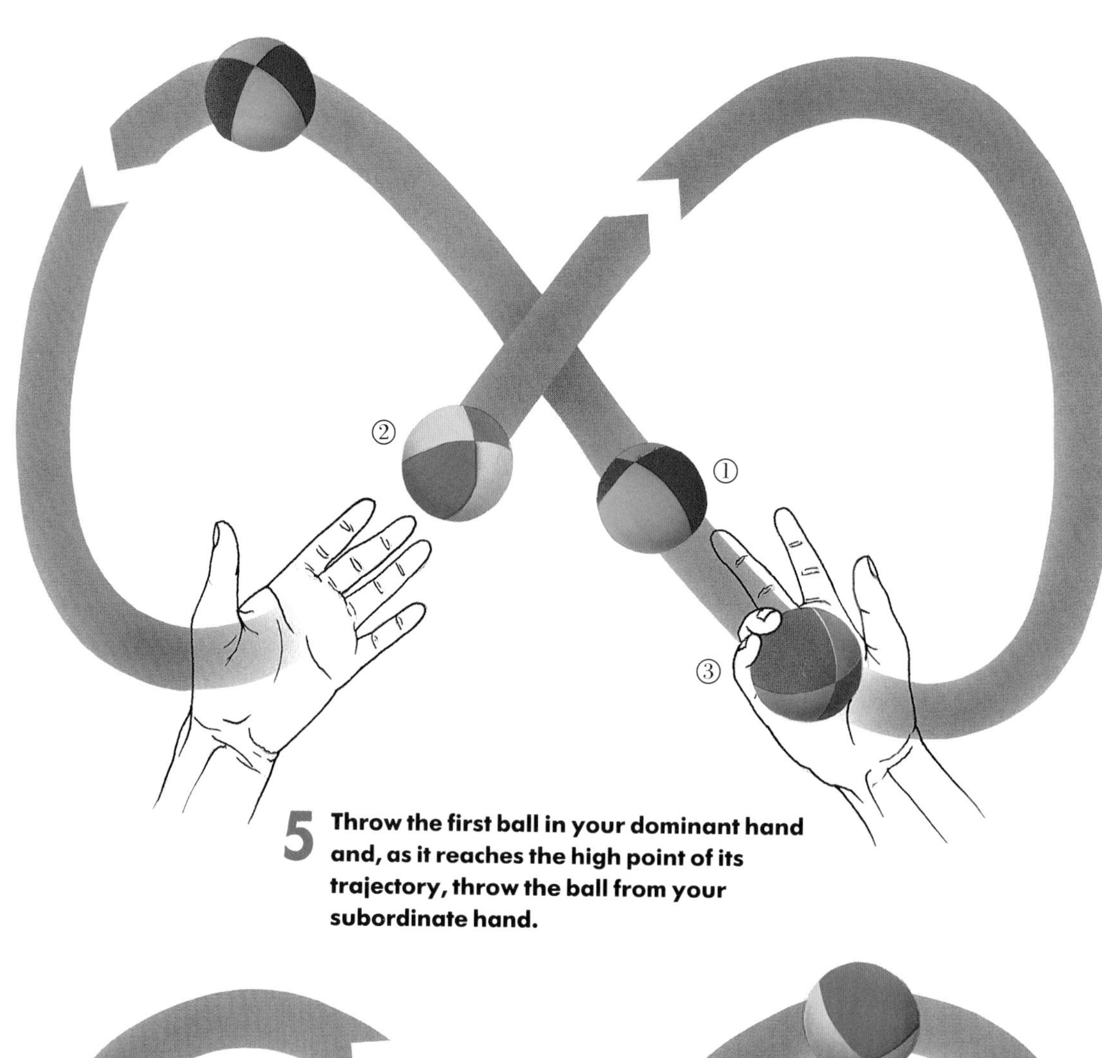

5 **Throw the first ball in your dominant hand and, as it reaches the high point of its trajectory, throw the ball from your subordinate hand.**

REMEMBER

- **Always start with the hand that is holding two balls.**
- **Every time a ball reaches the high point of its trajectory, throw the next ball.**
- **Always use a scooping, underhand throw.**
- **Say "Right-left right-left" (or "Left-right") as you throw, or count out loud.**
- **Do not watch the paths of the balls; concentrate on the peaks.**
- **Keep the underlying figure-eight pattern.**
- **Do not throw the balls forward.**
- **Stop cleanly by catching the last ball.**

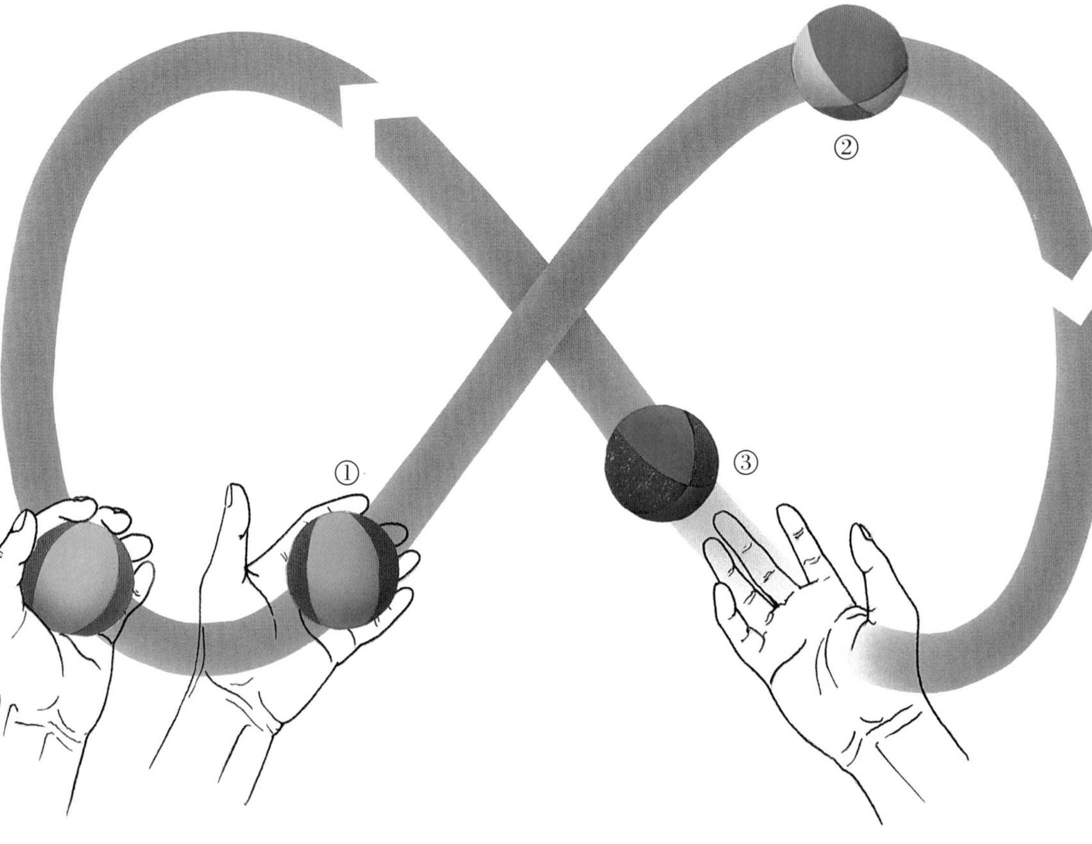

6 **Catch the first ball in your subordinate hand and, as the second ball reaches the high point of its trajectory, throw the third ball from your dominant hand. You will have to allow it to roll forward to your fingertips before you can throw it.**

Catch the second ball in your dominant hand and the third ball in your subordinate hand. Stop.

The two balls from your dominant hand should now be in your subordinate hand; the other ball, from your subordinate hand, should be in your dominant hand. Repeat the steps, saying "One-two-three-stop" as you perform each action, until you have mastered the movements.

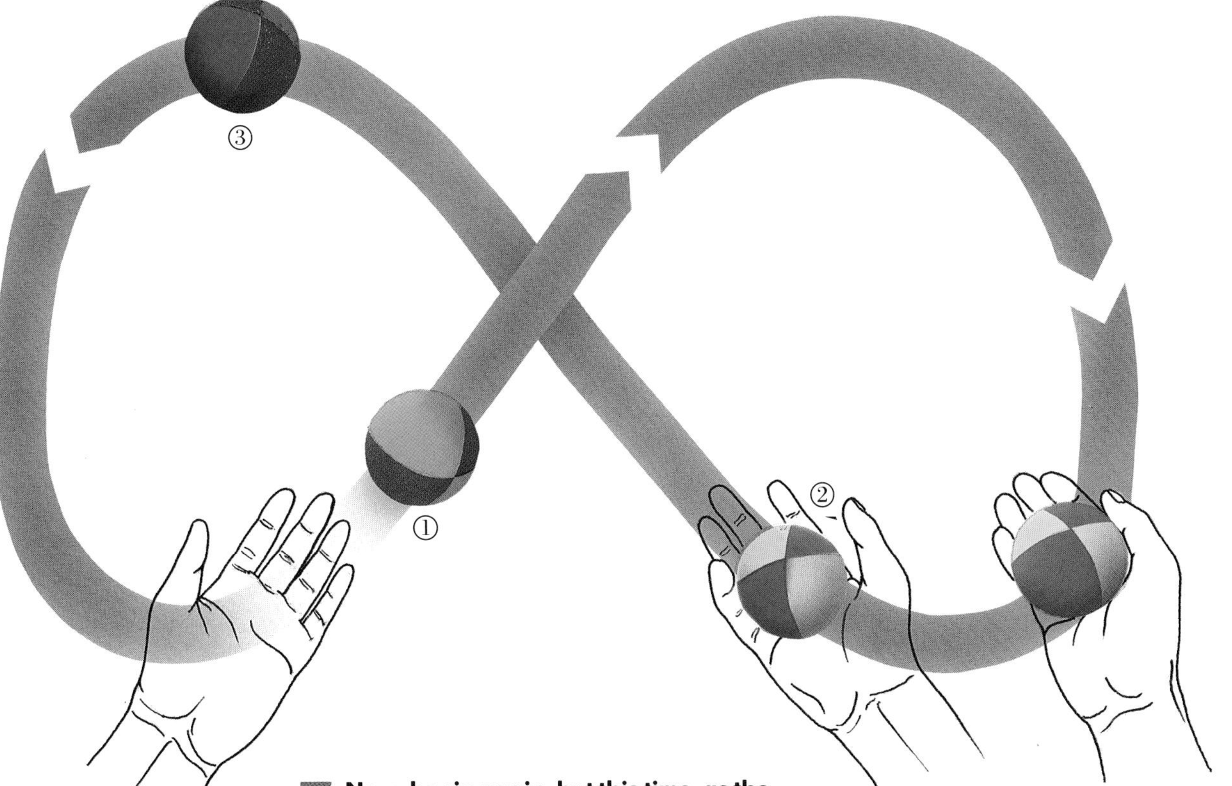

7 Now, begin again, but this time, as the third ball reaches the high point of its trajectory, throw the first ball from your subordinate hand. Keep on throwing, and you are juggling.

You will probably find it helpful to count as you throw to help establish and reinforce a rhythm. To keep going, you must be consistent with your throws. Keep your imaginary frame in your mind's eye and aim to throw into the top corners – no higher and no lower. When you have gotten control of the basic cascade pattern, practice looking through the pattern, focusing on a distant wall. Eventually you will be able to juggle without watching the balls all the time, just seeing the peaks of the trajectories with your peripheral vision, and you will be able to give up counting.

Once you can juggle in a cascade pattern, change the shape of your imaginary frame, making it wider or lower or higher. The higher you throw, the longer will be the interval between each catch, although gravity being what it is, a throw that is twice as high as normal will not give you twice as long between throwing and catching. Bear in mind, too, that the higher you throw, the farther you will have to move your hands to catch, because the accuracy of your throw will diminish over the greater distance.

At first, guard against throwing too fast. All that will happen is that all three balls will be in the air at once, and you will probably drop them all. Take things slowly, pausing between throws if necessary and remembering that the cue for the next throw is the peak of the previous throw. Only when you feel confident should you try to increase the speed by reducing the height of your throws. This is a valuable exercice in itself, but it also increases your dexterity and improves your hand-eye coordination.

TIPS

Not many people manage to juggle successfully on the first attempt – most people find that their hands and brains seem to want to do different things. If you are having problems, you may find the following points helpful.

- **Remember that for most of the time only one ball is in the air. The other two balls are either just entering or just leaving your hands.**
- **Go back to the two-ball action and try to visualize it with three balls.**
- **Work through the movements with three balls, but make no attempt to catch them, concentrating instead on the routine and rhythm of throwing.**
- **If you are tending to throw the balls forward so that you have to move to catch them, which will disrupt your rhythm, try standing in front of a wall and, making a definite scooping movement, concentrate on making the balls peak at a uniform distance from the wall.**
- **Make a determined effort to begin the cascade pattern with two balls in your subordinate hand. The ideal is to be able to start and finish the movement with either hand, and starting and finishing with two balls in your subordinate hand will both strengthen that hand and improve your overall coordination.**

The Shower

The shower is a pattern in which the props follow each other around in circles. Unlike the cascade, two balls are in the air most of the time rather than just one, and one hand does all the throwing while the other hand does all the catching. Accuracy and speed are the keys to success in this movement, and you should begin by practicing with just two balls.

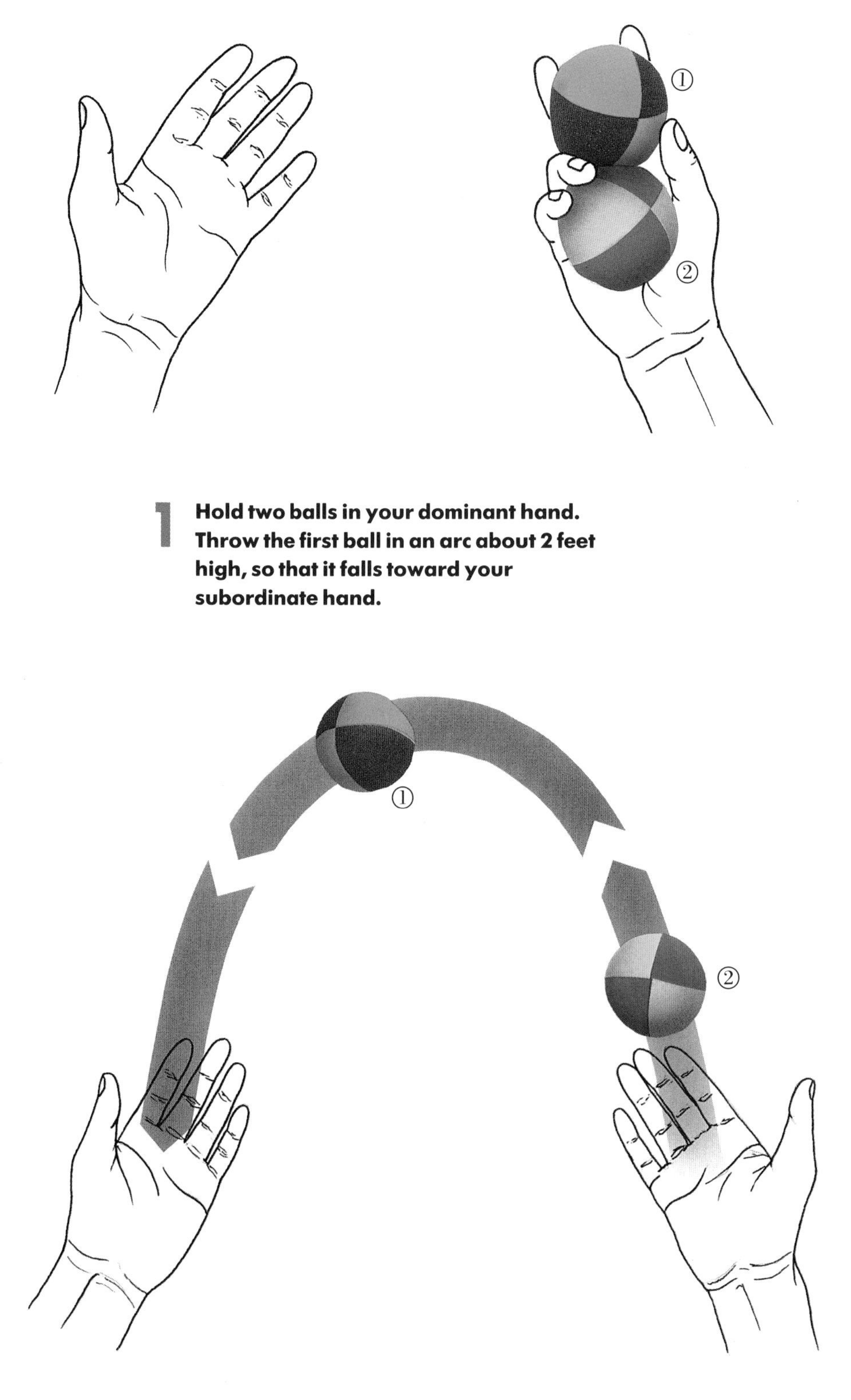

1 **Hold two balls in your dominant hand. Throw the first ball in an arc about 2 feet high, so that it falls toward your subordinate hand.**

2 **Almost immediately, throw the second ball; it should be well on its way when the first ball lands.**

The rhythm to build up is "Throw-throw-catch-catch."

The next step is to introduce the third ball.

REMEMBER

- Keep your eyes on the top of the arc so that you can judge where the ball falling toward your subordinate hand is going to land.
- The pass from subordinate to dominant hand is done outside your line of vision, so you have to bring your hands together.
- Every time a ball lands in your subordinate hand, pass it immediately to your dominant hand.
- Speed and accuracy are of the essence – the first two throws must follow in rapid succession to give you time to pass the third ball to your dominant hand, and every throw must be identical, or you will not be able to build up the rhythm.

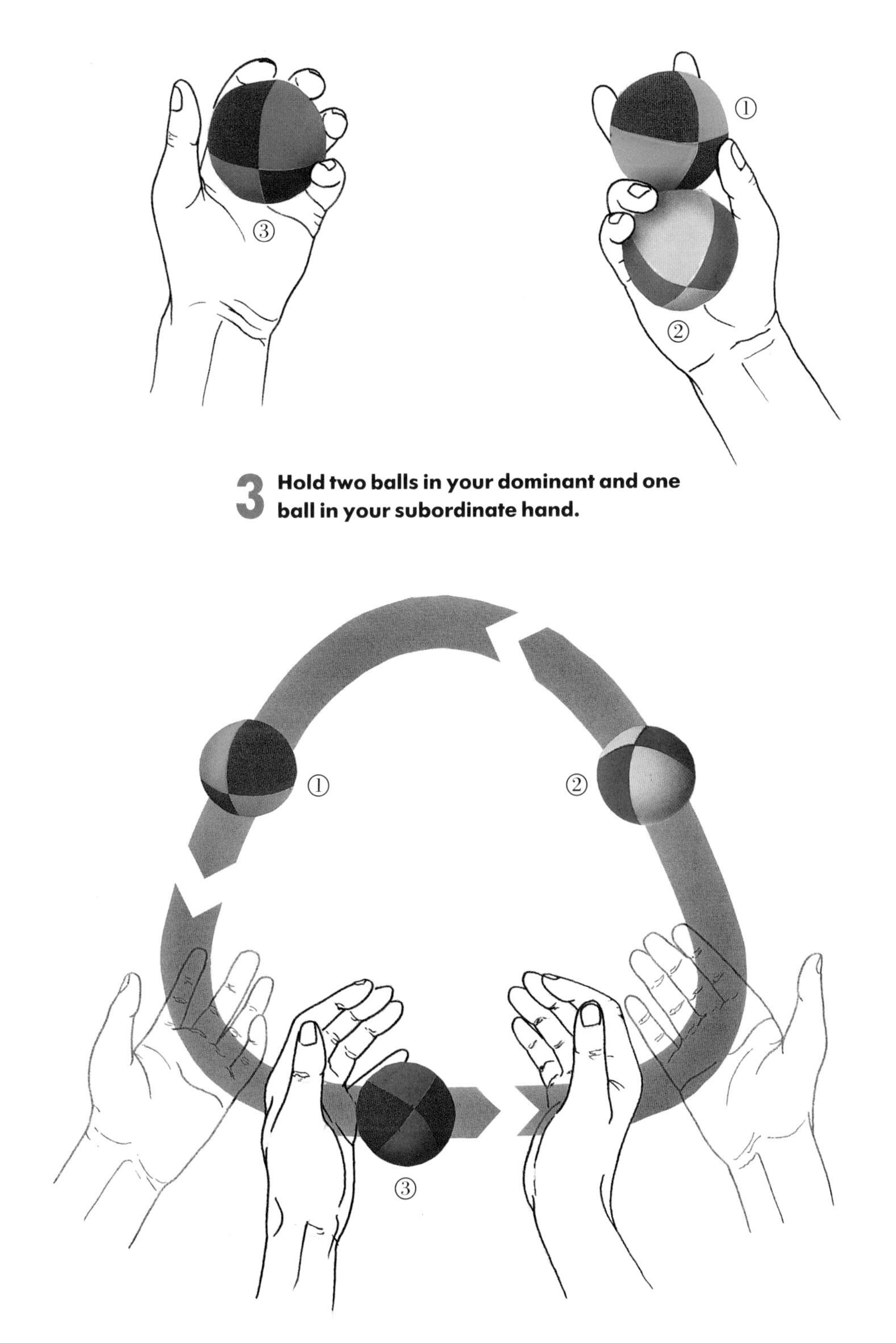

3 **Hold two balls in your dominant and one ball in your subordinate hand.**

4 **Throw the first ball, followed almost immediately by the second ball, in an arc toward your subordinate hand.**

As the second ball is leaving your dominant hand, pass the third ball from your subordinate hand to your dominant hand and immediately throw it in the arc.

The rhythm you are aiming for is "Throw-throw-pass-throw-catch-catch-catch." Once you have achieved that stage, the next step is to try to keep the movement going. Start in the same way, but every time a ball lands in your subordinate hand, pass it across to your dominant hand and throw it in an arc.

Because the shower is a movement that relies on one hand to do all the throwing, it is especially valuable to be able to do it with your subordinate hand. At first, you will probably spend more time picking up the balls that shoot all over the place, but persevere – it will be worth the effort.

The shower is more complicated than the cascade, but some people find that the movement comes naturally to them. Learning the shower can be a problem if you have already learned the cascade, but part of the fun and challenge of juggling lies in learning a movement until it becomes a habit and then deliberately breaking that habit by introducing a new pattern or variation.

Columns

In this pattern, the props rise and fall parallel to each other instead of crossing each others' paths. Another difference is that your hand should move toward the descending ball, rather than waiting for the ball to be thrown into the hand.

Before you can juggle with three balls, you must master the following two-ball movements. These three two-balls-in-one-hand patterns are effective movements in themselves and are also excellent exercises for your subordinate hand.

In all these movements you must keep the balls on a single plane in front of you – height and width are the crucial dimensions, not depth. It is very easy to "shovel" the balls toward your body, but you must make an effort to keep moving from side to side only.

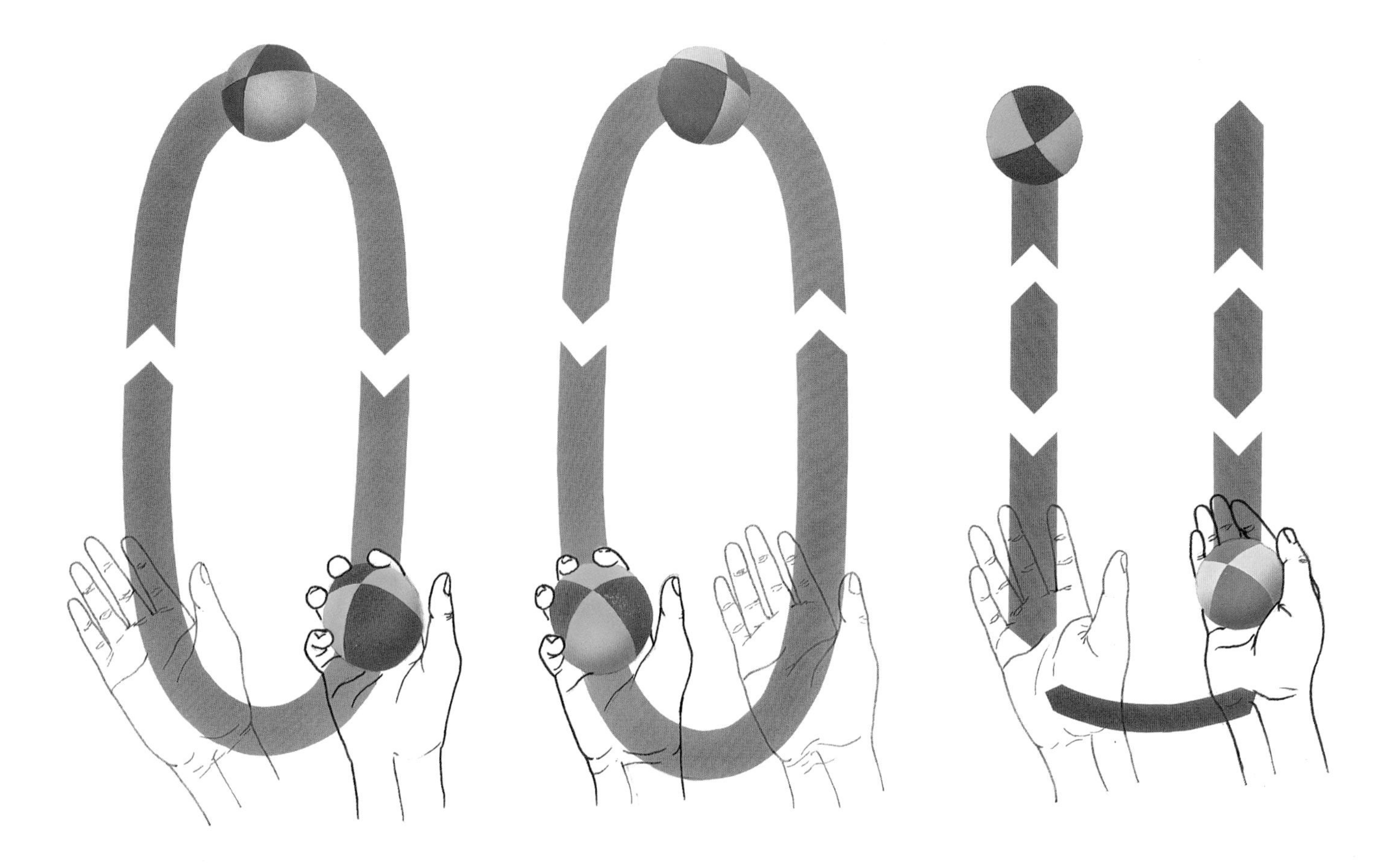

Inward Scoop

1 Hold two balls in one hand. Throw one ball up a little to one side – that is, if you started with the balls in your right hand, throw the first ball slightly to the right. As soon as the first ball peaks, throw the second one and move your hand to catch the first one. Scoop inward to throw the first ball, immediately returning your hand to catch the second ball. Continue in this way.

Outward Scoop

2 This movement is the same as the inward scoop except that instead of moving your hand slightly to one side of your body, you move it across your body – that is, if you start with the balls in your right hand, you should throw them up and slightly to your left, scooping outward to throw the returning ball.

The Column

3 In this movement, your hand moves on a horizontal plane, throwing and catching the balls, which travel in parallel lines. Every time a ball peaks, throw the other one.

When you can do these three movements with equal facility with either hand, you are ready to try the three-ball column.

Three-ball Column

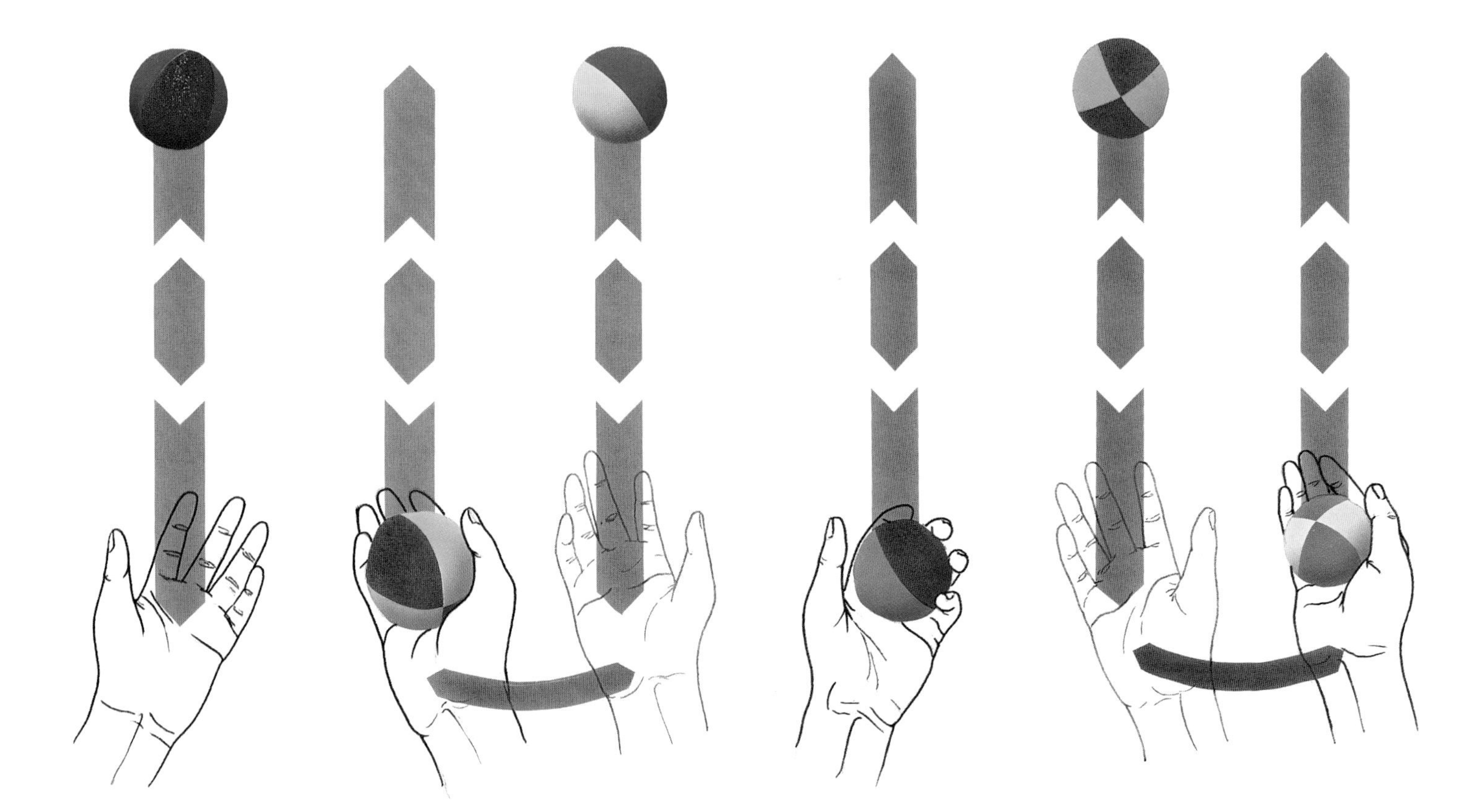

1 **Hold two balls in your dominant hand and one ball in your subordinate hand. Throw the first ball from your dominant hand straight up. As it peaks, move your dominant hand slightly to one side and throw the second ball, at the same time throwing the third ball, which is in your subordinate hand. The second and third balls are thus thrown at the same time, one on either side of the first ball.**

2 **Move your dominant hand to catch the first ball and immediately throw it again. Move your dominant hand into position to catch the second ball, at the same time catching the third ball with your subordinate hand.**

Continue in this way so that your dominant hand is moving to and fro, throwing and catching the first and second balls while the third ball moves parallel to, and at the same time as, the second ball. With this movement, your dominant hand is doing double work, actually juggling with two balls; your subordinate hand is merely throwing and catching one ball.

An alternative is to begin by throwing the second and third balls – that is, throw a ball from each hand simultaneously and then, when they peak, throw the remaining ball up between them.

As with all other juggling movements, practice columns with two balls in your subordinate hand and one in your dominant hand.

Practice, Progress, and Confidence Building

When you have all three patterns under control, practice them by varying the height and width of the pattern. This is especially useful with the cascade.

When you are juggling the cascade, showers, and columns successfully standing still, you could try moving around a little. All you have to do is remember to throw the balls in the direction you want to move. Try throwing one ball directly over your head, quite high, and turning through 180 degrees before resuming the pattern.

One of the best ways of practicing and of reinforcing a pattern is to teach it to someone else. You will probably learn far more during the process than your pupil.

ADVANCED THREE-BALL JUGGLING

The movements in this chapter are variations on the three basic patterns. There are literally hundreds of versions, but the ones described here are the most widely known and the most easily accomplished. Once you have mastered them, you will be able to use them as the basis for some quite complex routines.

As with the basic cascade, shower, and columns, you will probably find it easier to use round beanbags to practice with, since they are more accurate when thrown.

Half-shower

Begin with one ball to establish the pattern.

1 Throw the ball up and over with an outward scoop action from your dominant hand, catching it in the subordinate hand.

2 Throw the ball up and over with an inward scoop action from your subordinate hand, catching it in the dominant hand.

Practice these two throws until you are certain you can mix the two scoop actions at will.

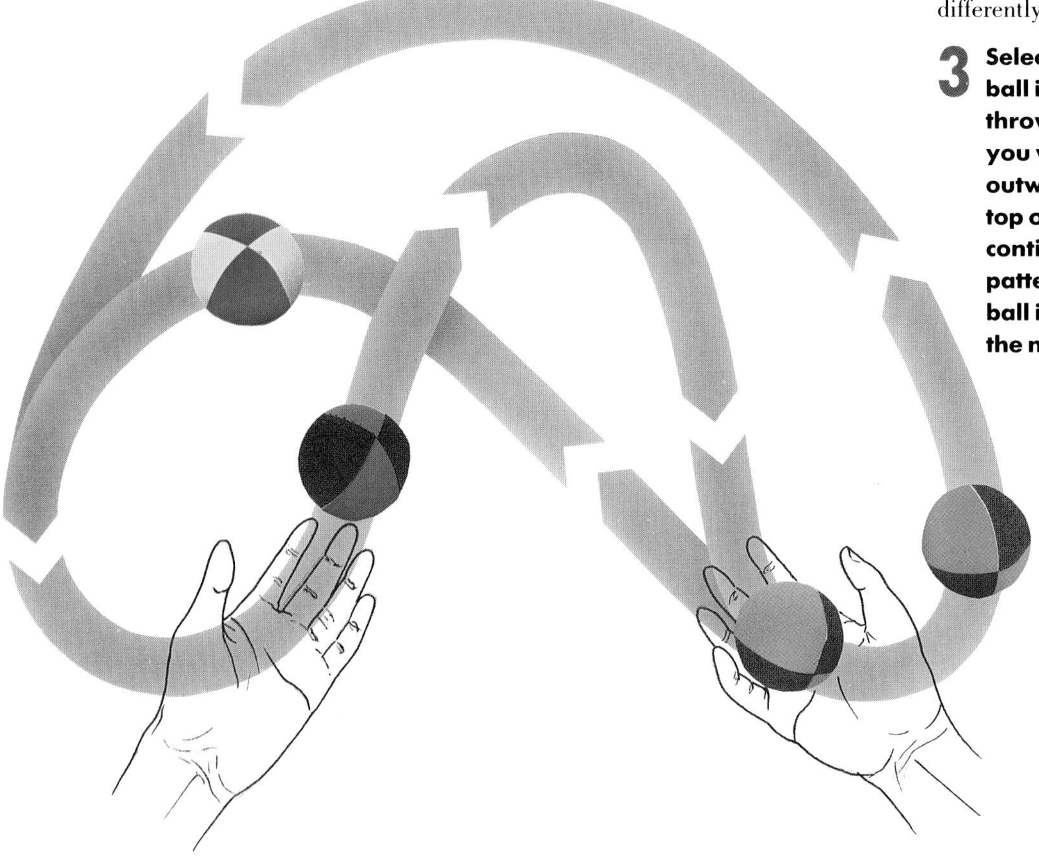

Now begin to juggle the cascade pattern with three differently colored balls.

3 **Select one of the colors and, when that ball is in your dominant hand, instead of throwing it with an inward scoop action as you would normally, throw it with an outward scoop so that it travels over the top of the other two balls, which should continue to move in the normal cascade pattern. As soon as you catch the selected ball in your subordinate hand, return it to the normal cascade pattern.**

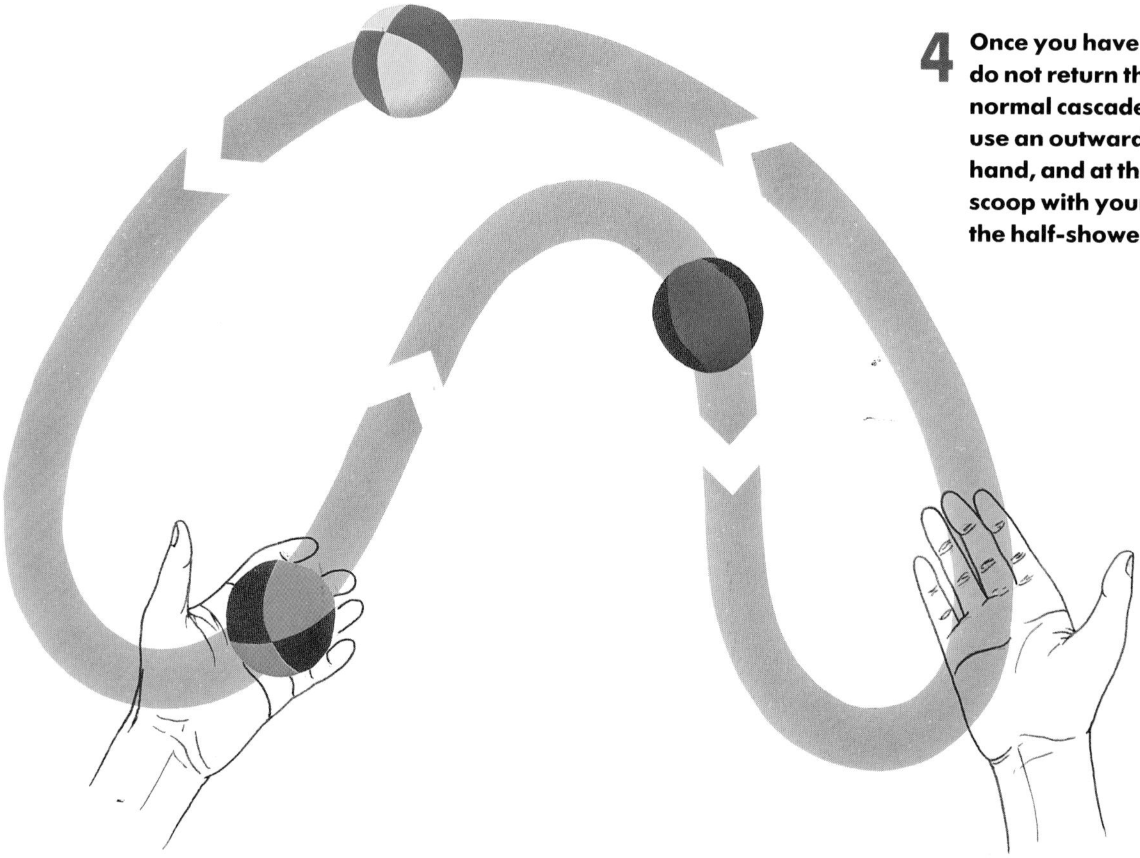

4 **Once you have mastered this movement, do not return the chosen ball to the normal cascade pattern, but continue to use an outward scoop with your dominant hand, and at the same time use an inward scoop with your subordinate hand. This is the half-shower pattern.**

REMEMBER

- **The peaks should be on the same side as the throws.**
- **Keep the palms of your hands upward.**

You should aim to throw the pattern as smoothly and rhythmically as possible, so it will look very impressive.

Practice using your subordinate hand to carry out the outward scoop movement. This is one of the best of all the routines for strengthening weak hands and for improving all-round agility and coordination.

Reverse-cascade

This variation on the basic cascade pattern involves throwing the balls continuously with an outward instead of an inward scoop – that is, you are throwing every ball over the incoming ball rather than under it. In the basic cascade pattern, you throw in an underhand motion from a point near the midline of your body, catching on the outside. In the reverse-cascade, you will be throwing from a point beside your body and at shoulder level, and catching near the midline. You will still, however, be following a figure-eight path.

You will inevitably find at first that, because the balls are being thrown over the incoming ones, you will tend to throw them higher and wider than you would normally. As you practice this pattern, you will be able to reduce both the height and the width until it takes up no more room than the basic cascade. Try to avoid throwing the ball so far over the top of the other balls' paths that your catching hand has to move away from your body to catch it. Ideally, you should catch the balls just in front of your trunk, at about waist height.

TIP

You might find it easier to keep your throws to a uniform height if you imagine that a small hoop, about the size of a circle made by your thumbs and forefingers, is suspended at eye-level in front of you. Aim to throw the balls so that they fall through this hoop.

1 Begin with one ball and practice throwing it with an overhand motion. Release the ball at shoulder height and catch it in your subordinate hand at about waist height. Repeat, throwing from your subordinate to your dominant hand.

When you feel comfortable throwing and catching one ball, take a ball in each hand.

2 Throw the first ball from your dominant hand. As soon as the first ball reaches the high point of its trajectory, throw the second ball from your subordinate hand so that the balls' paths cross in mid-air and the balls change hands.

Repeat the action, concentrating on the peaks.

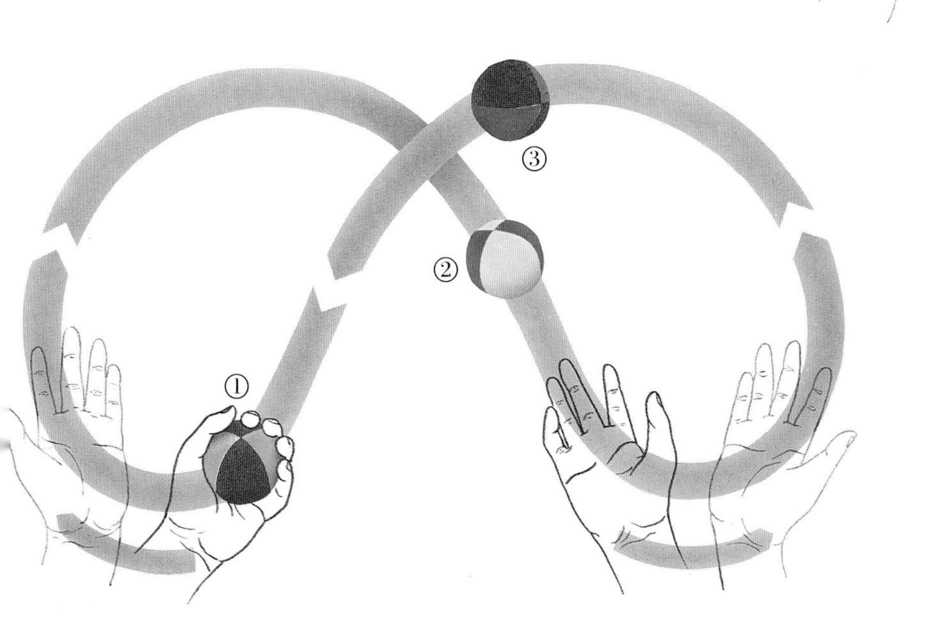

3 Using three balls, when each ball peaks, throw another one over it and just keep going.

A common mistake is to revert to the underhand throw. You must concentrate on catching on the inside and scooping toward the outside. You might also find at first that the pattern widens so that the throws are uncatchable. You can avoid this by practicing making the throws small, and by remembering that the peak of each throw is on the same side of your body as the throw itself and that the ball will fall toward the midline of your body.

Overhead Cascade

Performing this trick requires more space above your head than is found in the normal room, and this is especially true if you attempt this pattern with rings or clubs.

Begin by lying on your back on the floor with three balls. Go through the process of learning the cascade, just as you did when you were learning the basic pattern – that is, begin with one ball, throwing it from hand to hand, then use two balls and, finally, three. Now stand up and begin to juggle the cascade pattern.

To revert to a regular pattern, toss a ball high into the air, point your fingers to the front, and continue.

As you gain confidence, you should be able to move from a standing position to kneeling to lying down and back again while you maintain the overhead cascade pattern continuously.

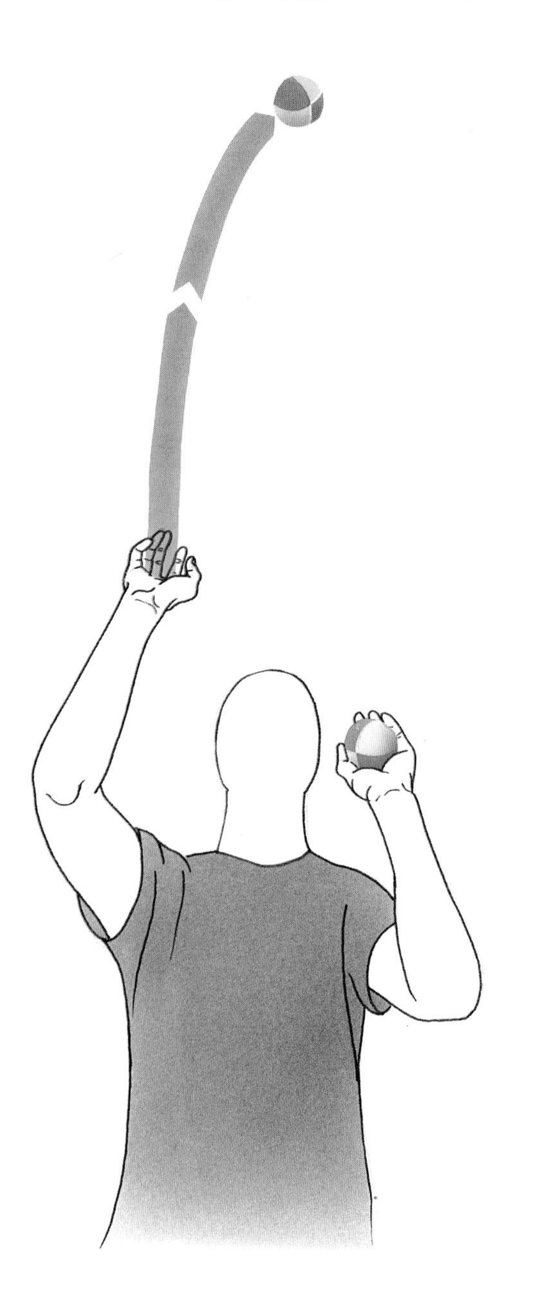

1 **Toss the first ball high into the air.**

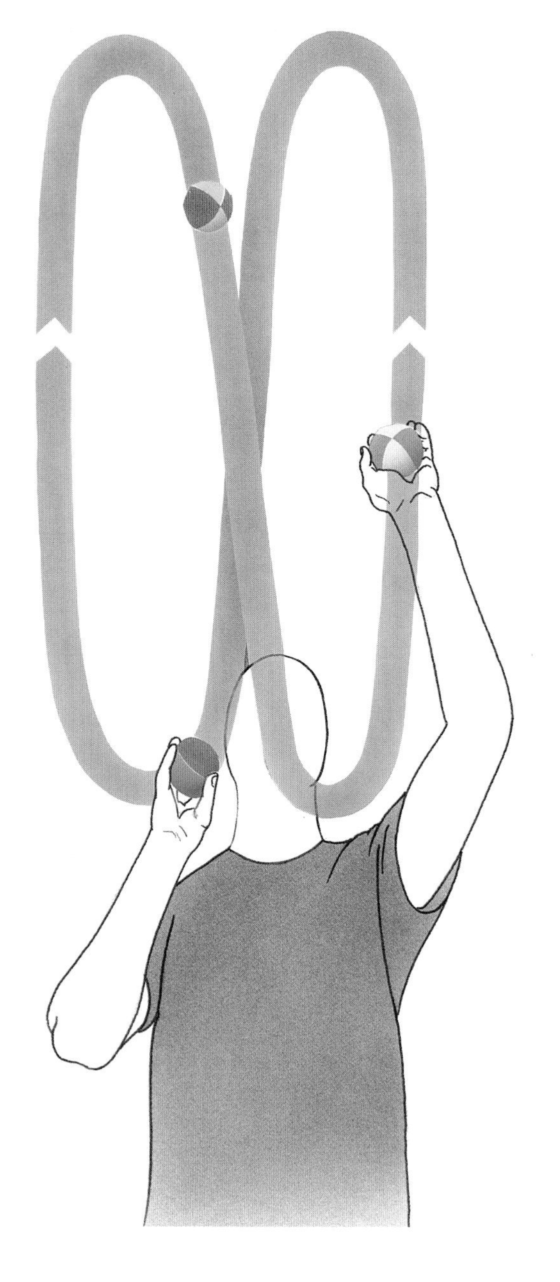

2 **Lean your head back and juggle as you did when you were lying on the floor, keeping your head back and your elbows up.**

If you find yourself throwing the balls too far forward, you probably need to lean back a little more.

Juggler's Tennis

Now that you are able to juggle the cascade (underhand throws and inward scoops) and the reverse-cascade (overhand throws and outward scoops), you should be able to combine the two patterns into juggler's tennis. You will need three differently colored balls, one of which is going to be the "tennis" ball. The aim is to juggle a cascade with two balls while the "tennis" ball is thrown backward and forward over the top.

To start with, however, practice juggling the cascade with your subordinate hand and the reverse-cascade with your dominant hand simultaneously – that is, juggle a half-shower. Then, use your dominant hand to juggle the cascade and your subordinate hand to juggle the reverse-cascade. Now you are ready to try juggler's tennis.

1 Begin juggling the cascade pattern, but every time the "tennis" ball comes to your dominant hand, toss it to your subordinate hand in a high throw.

2 When the "tennis" ball comes to your subordinate hand, toss it to your dominant hand.

3 Continue to juggle a cascade pattern with the other two balls.

When you have mastered the basic pattern, you will be able to vary the height to which you throw the "tennis" ball. At first, confine yourself to tossing the ball over the "net" with little throws. Eventually, however, you should be able to toss the "tennis" ball fairly high – throwing lobs and smashes – while the cascade pattern with the other two balls continues uninterrupted underneath.

Three-ball Flash

This is an important pattern to learn if you want to progress to juggling with five balls (see Chapter 4). During the pattern, all three balls are in the air at the same time, leaving your hands empty for a fraction of a second – in which you clap them before catching the balls and resuming the pattern.

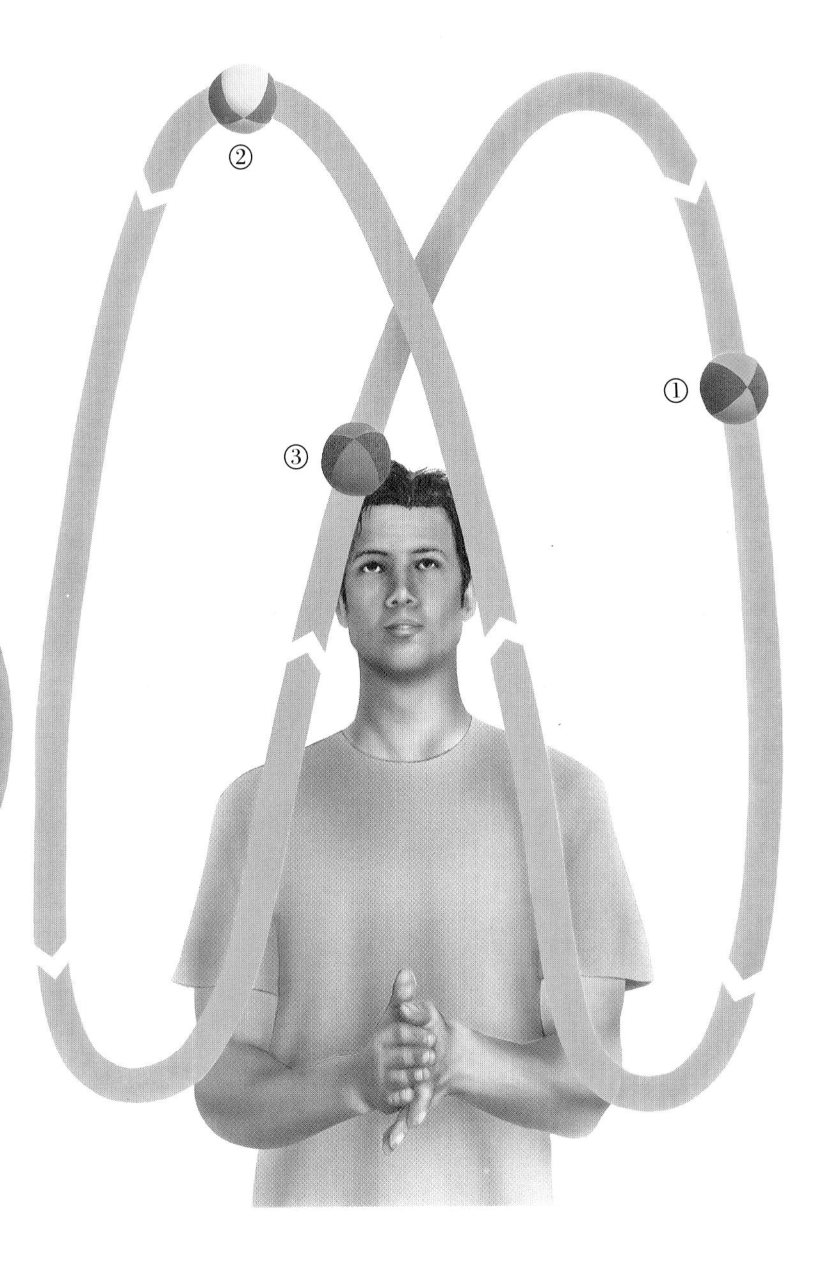

1 Begin juggling the cascade pattern, but throw the balls higher and faster than usual. When you have built up a rhythm – "Right-left-right" – try to clap your hands before catching them – "Left-right-left."

When you feel more confident, you might try pirouetting – i.e., turning through 360 degrees – while the balls are, apparently, suspended in mid-air.

You should also practice this pattern beginning with your subordinate hand.

Columns Variations

The two most popular variations of the columns pattern are the dummy and the yo-yo. These one-handed juggling patterns are relatively easy to perform, but they look quite complicated, and it can take an audience several moments to realize just what is going on!

The Dummy

In this pattern, you juggle two balls in one hand, but instead of throwing and catching the third ball with the other hand, you simply hold it in that hand, moving the ball up and down.

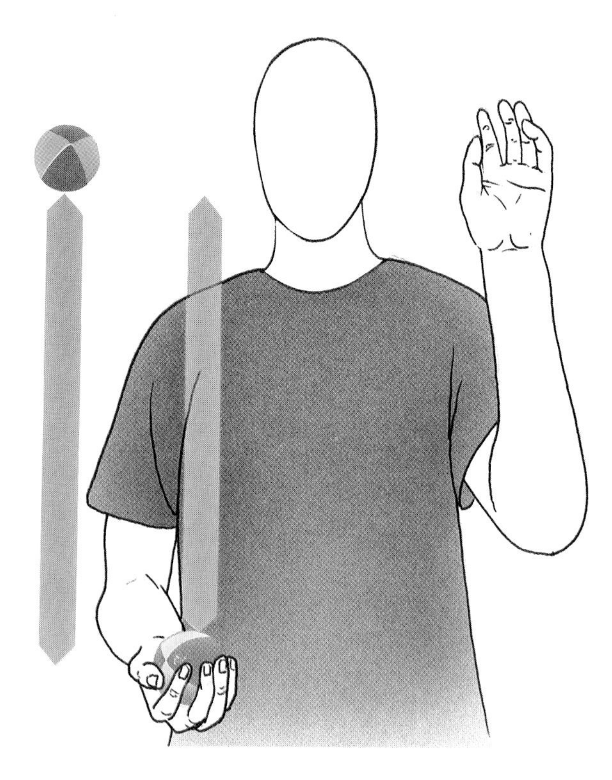

1 Juggle two balls in columns with your dominant hand, keeping the balls on their own paths. Hold your subordinate hand out so that you can see it. Don't move it yet – just get used to seeing it.

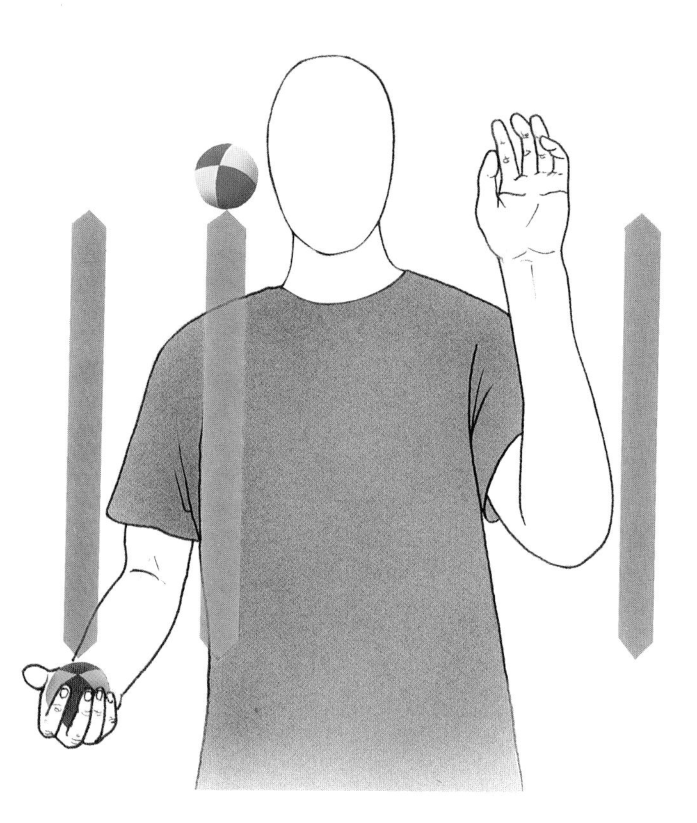

2 Select one of the balls in your dominant hand and, every time you throw it, raise your subordinate hand, mimicking the movement of the chosen ball with your empty hand.

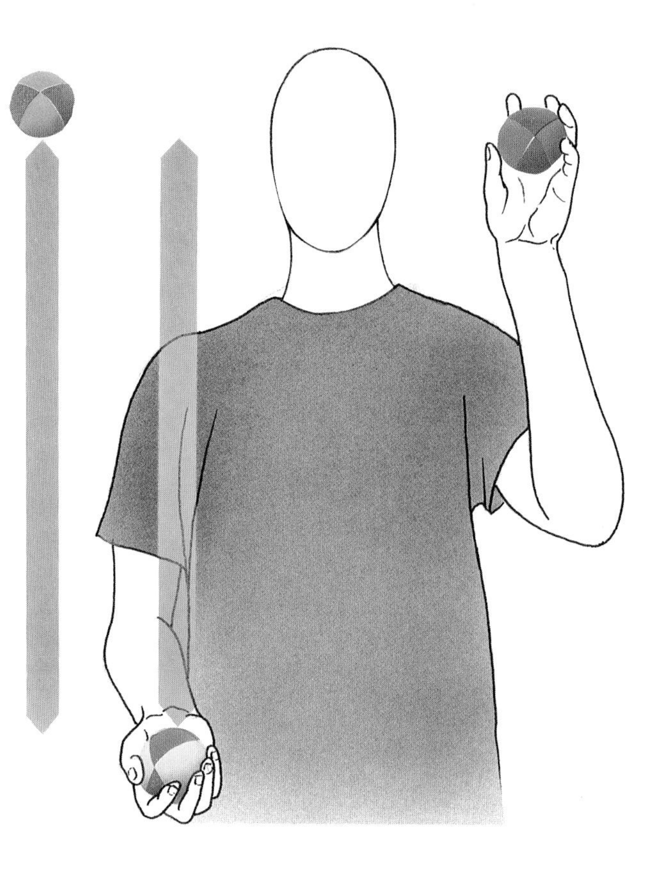

3 Now, take a ball in your subordinate hand. Do not throw or catch it, simply move it up and down synchronously with the chosen ball being juggled by your dominant hand, holding the ball so that it can be clearly seen by your audience.

When this trick is done well, it will take some time for your audience to realize that this third ball is not being thrown but moved up and down in your hand.

THE YO-YO

This is very similar to the dummy, but you should hold the third ball about 6 inches above the innermost of the two balls being juggled in your dominant hand.

1 **Move your hand up and down, keeping the third ball the same distance from the inner ball so that it looks as if the lower ball is joined to it by a piece of string.**

ASSORTED VARIATIONS

Once your have mastered the basic columns pattern (see Chapter 1), try catching the middle ball with your subordinate hand instead of the dominant one. Then control the middle ball with alternate hands. When you have gotten used to doing this, you will be able to move the middle ball around, to the right or the left of the other two balls.

The possible variations are almost endless. Watch other jugglers and you will pick up ideas for new movements – as well as being able to understand how they have built up their routines.

Shower Variations

THE STATUE OF LIBERTY

This variation on the shower pattern is created by throwing balls upward to your extended arms and allowing them to drop straight down, to be caught and thrown again. You must throw the balls very accurately so that they drop neatly into your subordinate hand from just above it.

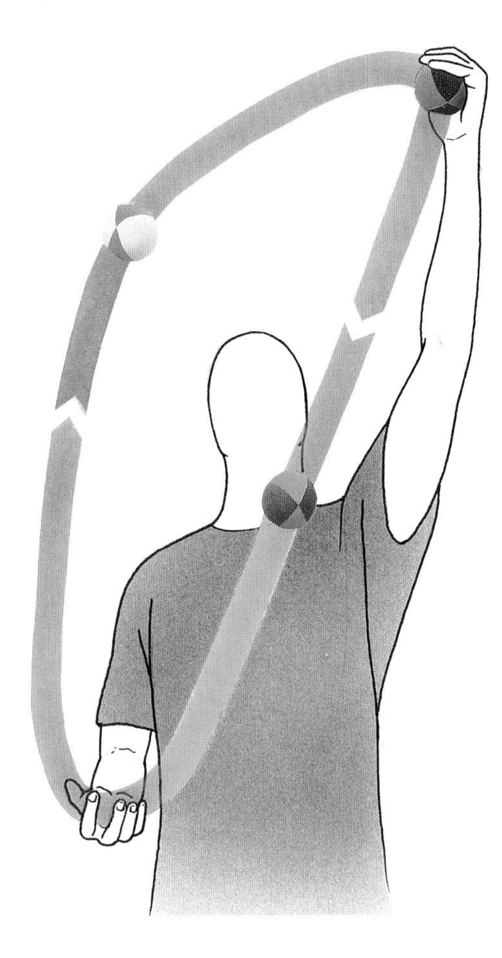

1 **Begin with two balls in your dominant hand and one ball in your subordinate hand, which is held high and 3–4 inches in front of you.**

Throw the balls from your dominant hand upward, one after the other. Drop the ball from your subordinate hand and catch the first ball from your dominant hand.

Continue in this way, throwing a ball every time it comes to the dominant hand and catching, then immediately dropping, a ball every time it comes to the subordinate hand. Keep your subordinate hand as still as possible.

The Seesaw

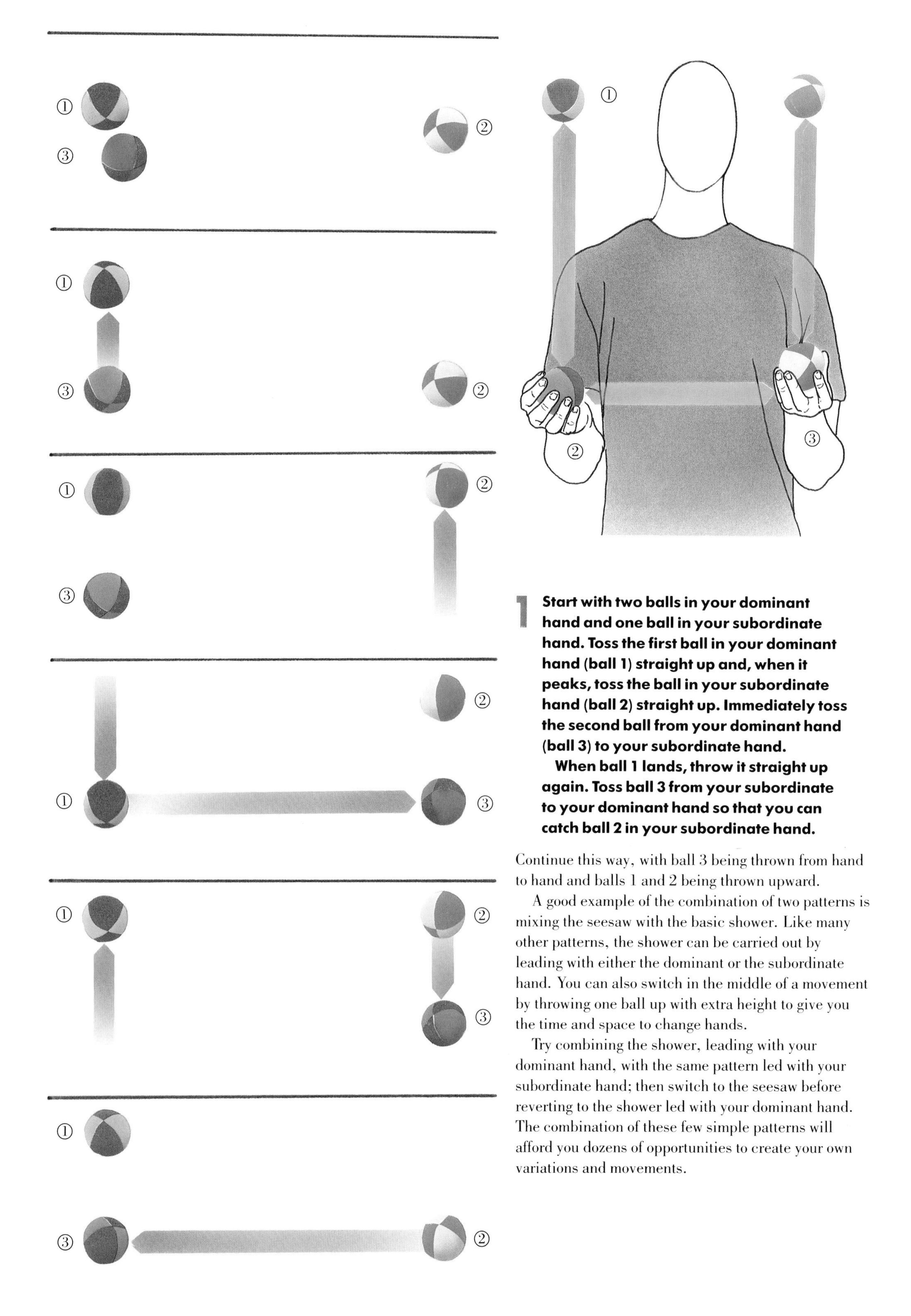

1 Start with two balls in your dominant hand and one ball in your subordinate hand. Toss the first ball in your dominant hand (ball 1) straight up and, when it peaks, toss the ball in your subordinate hand (ball 2) straight up. Immediately toss the second ball from your dominant hand (ball 3) to your subordinate hand.

When ball 1 lands, throw it straight up again. Toss ball 3 from your subordinate to your dominant hand so that you can catch ball 2 in your subordinate hand.

Continue this way, with ball 3 being thrown from hand to hand and balls 1 and 2 being thrown upward.

A good example of the combination of two patterns is mixing the seesaw with the basic shower. Like many other patterns, the shower can be carried out by leading with either the dominant or the subordinate hand. You can also switch in the middle of a movement by throwing one ball up with extra height to give you the time and space to change hands.

Try combining the shower, leading with your dominant hand, with the same pattern led with your subordinate hand; then switch to the seesaw before reverting to the shower led with your dominant hand. The combination of these few simple patterns will afford you dozens of opportunities to create your own variations and movements.

Carrying and Placing Variations

Instead of throwing a ball to a particular point, you can carry it before dropping it, passing it, or throwing it to the other hand. Here are four possible variations for you to try.

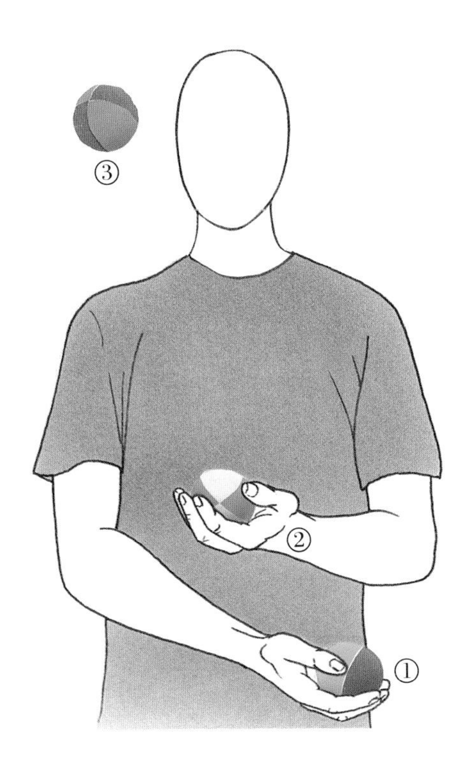

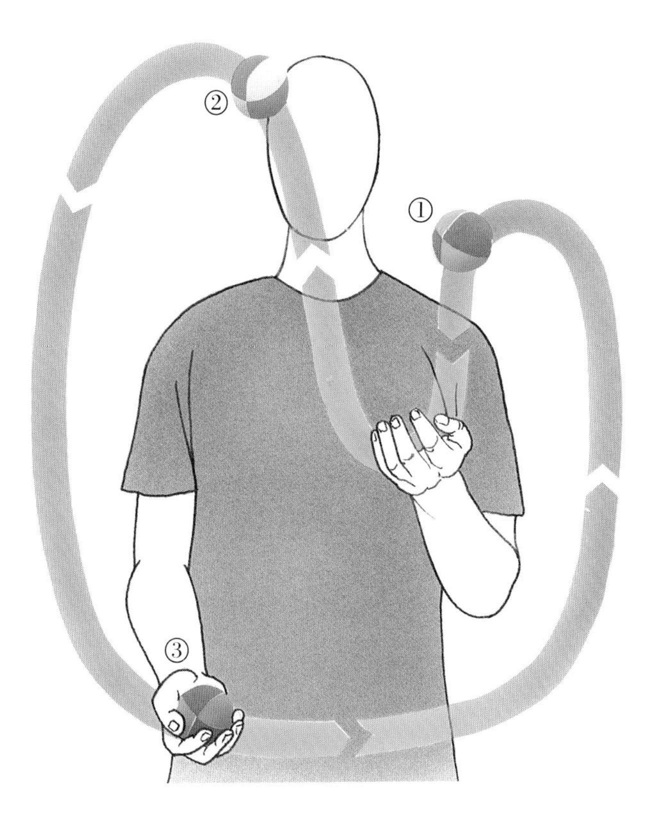

1 **Carry the ball across your body under your opposite arm and toss it straight up into the pattern.**

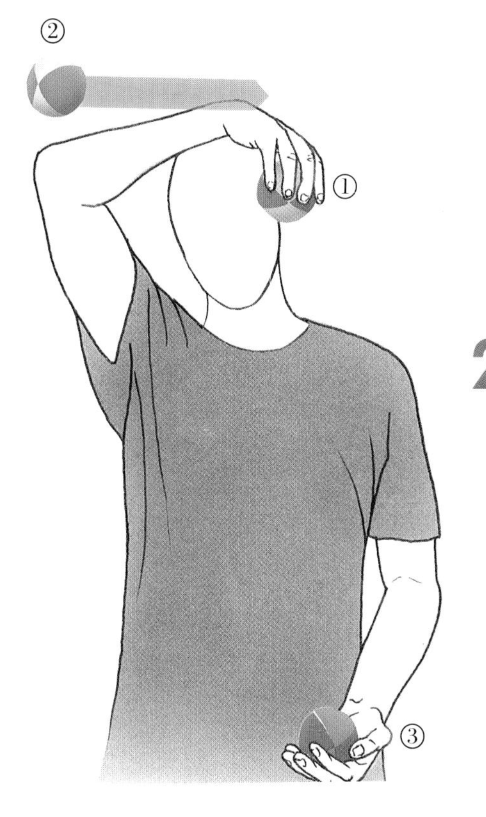

2 **Carry the first ball across the top of the pattern and drop it straight down into the movement. As soon as you drop the first ball, reach across and, palm down, catch the second ball. Meanwhile, you will have thrown the third ball and caught the first ball. Carry the second ball across the top of the pattern and drop it, reaching over quickly to catch the third ball. Continue in this way.**

② ①

③

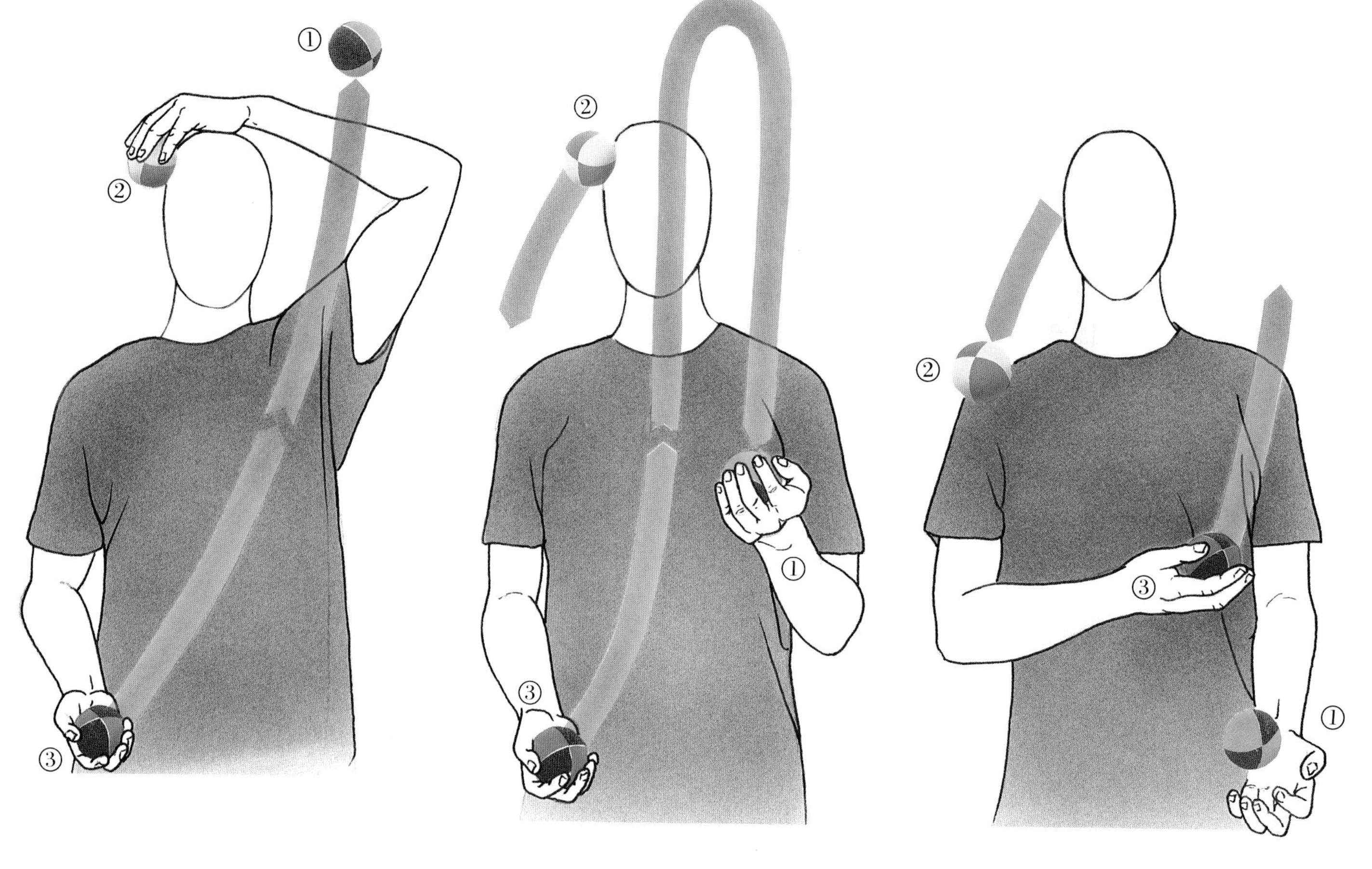

3 Place the ball on your head and let it drop into the pattern.

4 Throw the first ball with your dominant hand and place the second ball on your head with your subordinate hand.

5 Reach back to catch the first ball with your subordinate hand; then throw the third ball under it, following the path of the first ball.

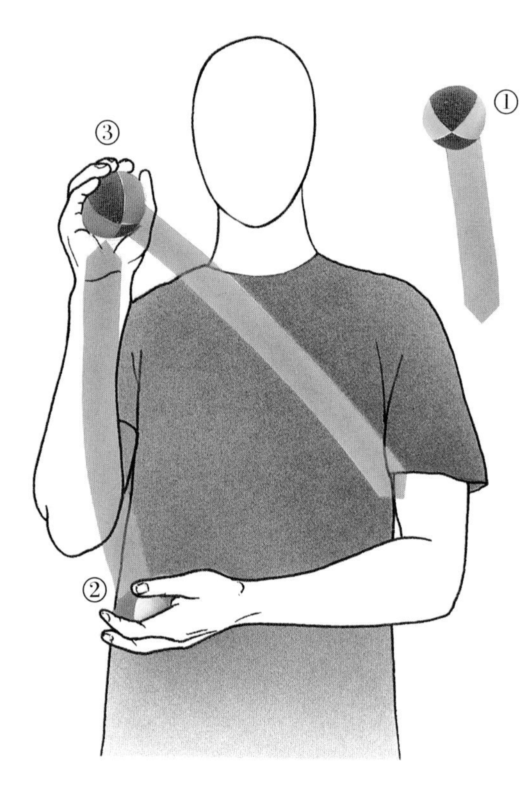

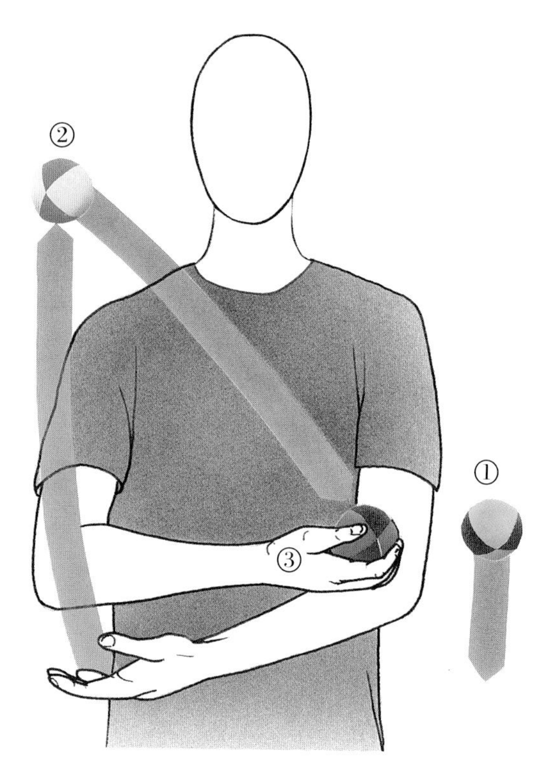

6 Begin a cascade pattern with three balls. Then, with your dominant hand, catch one ball (ball 1) higher in the air than usual. Bring it down across your body in a slicing movement before throwing it.

7 So that ball 2 is not hit as it is thrown from your subordinate hand by your dominant hand, scoop your subordinate hand farther to your dominant side so that ball 2 can be thrown under your dominant hand. The higher you throw ball 2, the more exaggerated and visually effective the slicing movement can be.

Practice all these patterns so that you can do them equally well with your subordinate hand.

The last example described here requires especially fast reflexes and accurate throwing, and perfecting it requires considerable effort and practice. However, it is a very effective pattern and well worth the effort you will have to make.

Crossed-arms Variations

There are several possible patterns that can be juggled with crossed arms. Perhaps the simplest is the reverse-cascade.

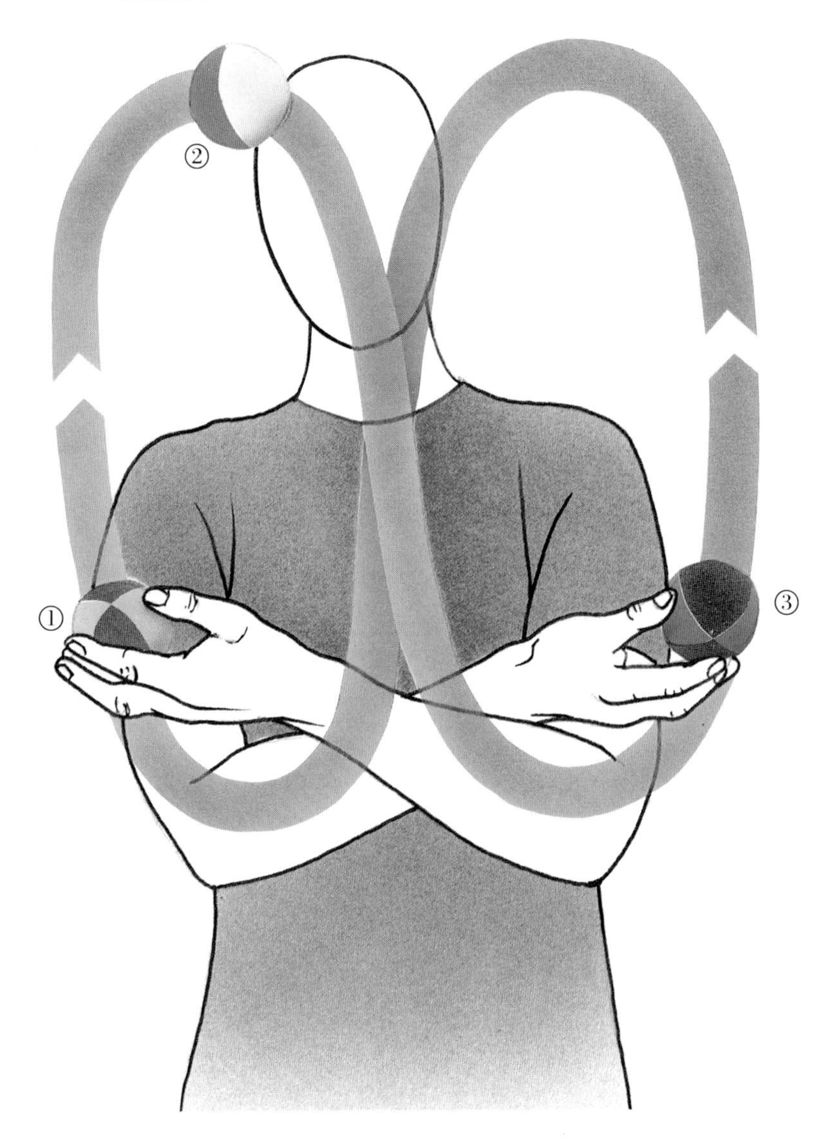

1 Begin by throwing one ball from hand to hand, then move on to two balls and, finally, to three.

Although this can look quite impressive by itself, it is best presented as part of a series of moves in which you cross and uncross your arms.

TIP

Remember to keep your juggling within two dimensions – height and width.

Another simple crossed-arm variation is based on juggler's tennis, but in this movement the "tennis" ball goes under the net.

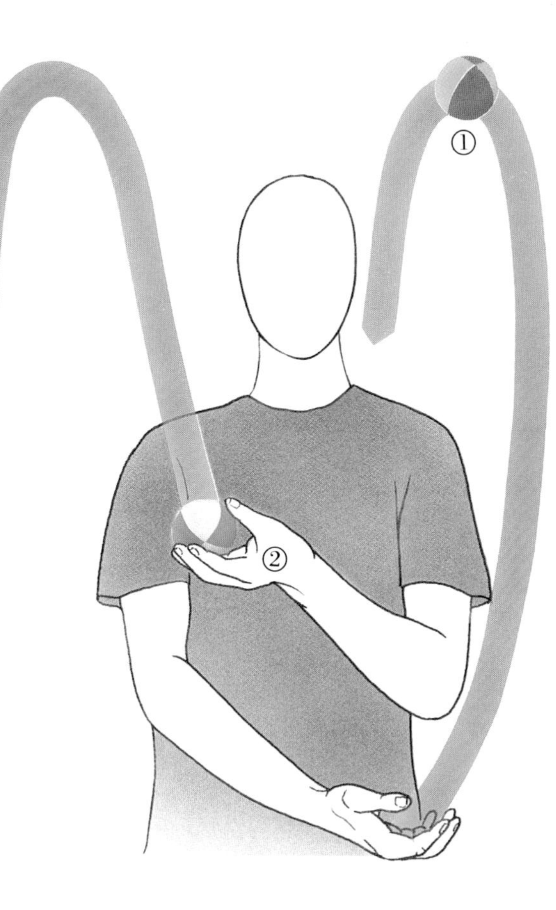

1 **Start with two balls, one in each hand, and cross your hands, dominant under subordinate.**

Throw the ball in your dominant hand straight up. Throw the ball in your subordinate hand up and across your body.

Uncross your hands and catch the first ball in your subordinate hand and the second ball in your dominant hand.

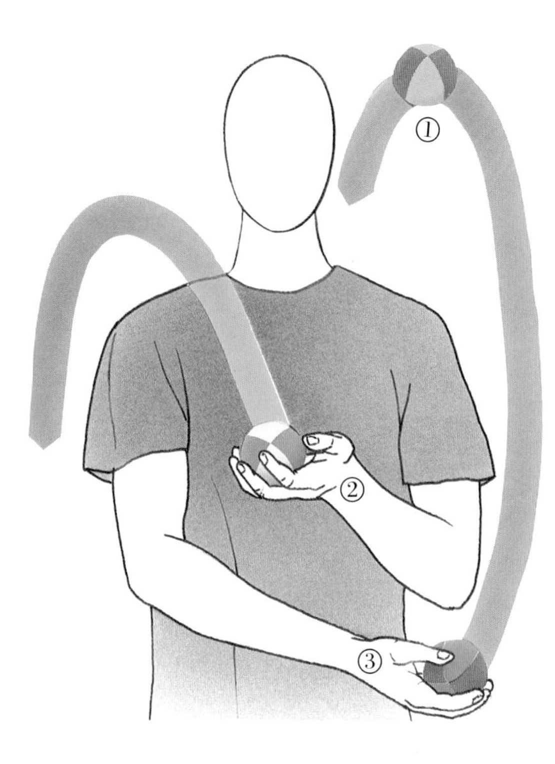

Practice these moves until you are ready to use three balls.

2 **Take two balls (balls 1 and 3) in your dominant hand and one ball (ball 2) in your subordinate hand.**

Cross your dominant hand under your subordinate hand and throw ball 1 straight up.

3 **Throw ball 2 up and across your body in a cascade pattern. As ball 2 peaks, throw ball 3 and begin juggling.**

Practice this routine, but begin with two balls in your subordinate hand and by crossing your subordinate hand under your dominant hand.

You should now be ready to play upside-down juggler's tennis. The "tennis" ball is carried under the pattern in one direction, caught and thrown straight up, and caught in the opposite hand. It is then carried under, thrown straight up on the other side, and caught in the opposite hand. In this way, the "tennis" ball describes a broad U-shape under the pattern made by the other two balls.

Body Shots

You can throw an occasional ball or a series of balls during a routine under or behind some part of your body to add variety to a pattern. The three most commonly seen variations are under the leg, behind the back, and over the shoulder. These body shots are ideal for mixing with all the basic patterns, and they do introduce an element of keep-fit into your juggling routines by demanding extra mobility, balance, and dexterity. They will also increase your confidence by encouraging you to continue juggling a pattern even when one of the balls is out of your line of sight, obscured by part of your body.

You should practice all three of these movements on both sides so that you can throw under your right and left leg or over your right and left shoulder with equal ease.

Under the Leg

One of the easiest tricks is to throw a ball under your leg while you are juggling.

1 You will have to raise the leg at the same side as the hand with which you are throwing moves to throw the ball – for example, raise your left leg and throw the ball in your left hand underneath it and up toward the usual point above your left hand.

You will find it quite difficult to perfect the timing of raising a leg and throwing a ball. You might find it easier to begin a juggling pattern in this way, throwing the first ball under your leg and then juggling in the pattern in the normal way. When you can do this easily, try throwing the ball under your leg in the middle of your pattern, balancing on one leg so that you can raise and lower the other leg without disrupting the rhythm of your pattern.

Eventually you should be able to toss successive throws under one leg or the other, even under each leg in turn.

Behind the Back

Begin with just one ball.

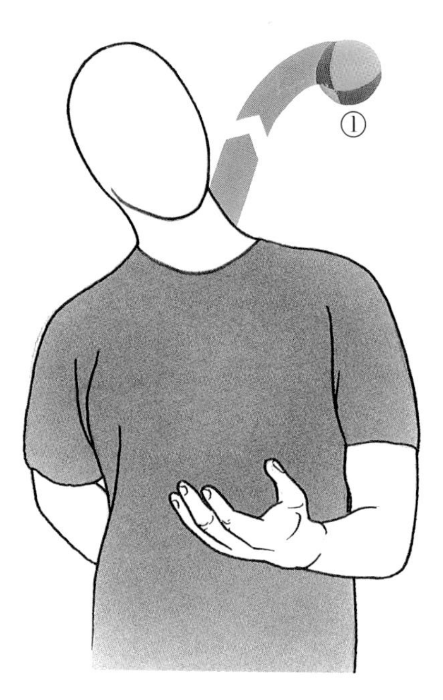

1 Throw it from your dominant hand, behind and across your back and over your opposite shoulder – that is, if you are beginning with your left hand, it should appear over your right shoulder – and catch it with your subordinate hand.
Now, try with two balls.

TIP

Practice turning your head from side to side and moving your arms into position without throwing any balls. Do this until you feel comfortable with the rhythm.

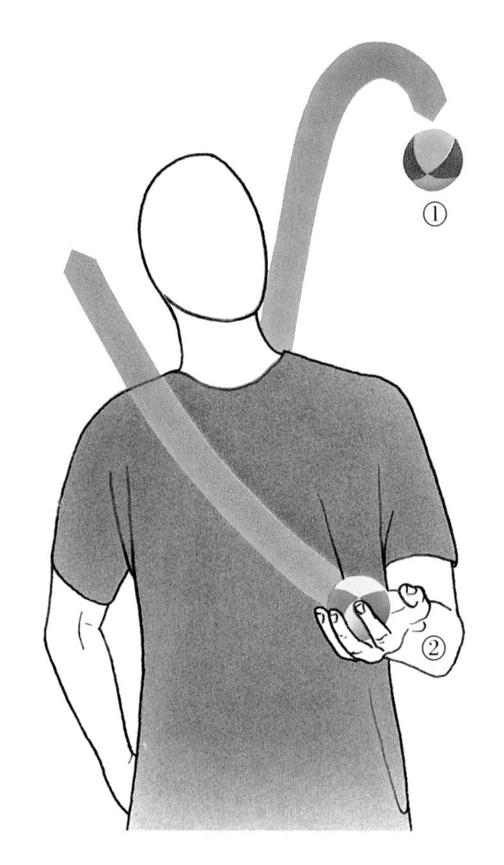

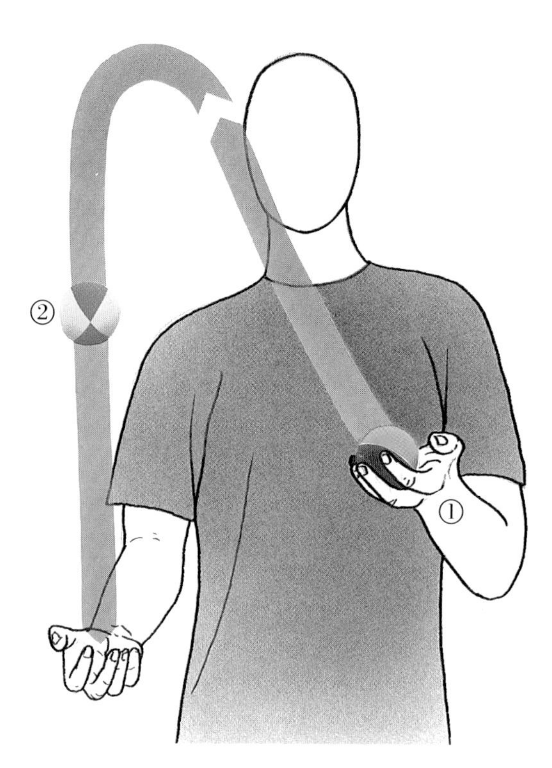

2 Take one ball in each hand and repeat the throw as before, beginning with your dominant hand. As the first ball appears over your shoulder, throw the ball that is in your subordinate hand.

3 Continue in a normal cascade pattern, catching the first ball in your subordinate hand.

When you feel confident with two balls, try juggling a cascade pattern with three balls.

REMEMBER

- **Practice with one ball and two balls until you can throw smoothly and accurately.**
- **Throw higher than you would normally to give yourself more time.**
- **All the catches are in the front, but your head is turned away from the side on which you catch the ball so you are, in effect, catching "blind."**
- **Your throws must be especially accurate to make catching easier.**
- **Reach as high as you can behind your back with your throwing hand.**

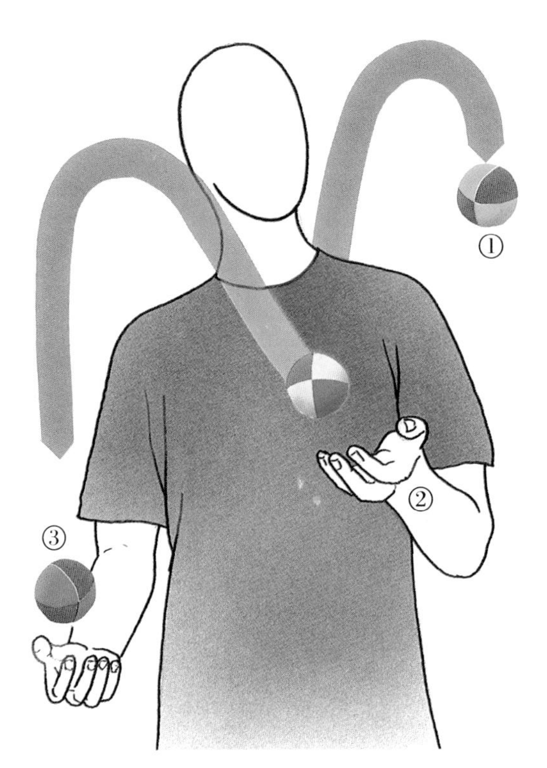

4 Select one ball – again, it is useful to have different colored balls – and when that ball comes into your dominant hand, reach behind your back, throw the ball up and across your back so that it comes over your shoulder to be caught by your subordinate hand and returned into the cascade pattern.

Because the path of the ball thrown behind your back is longer than the paths of the other balls, you must pause slightly before your next throw.

When you throw with your dominant hand up and over the shoulder on your subordinate side, turn your head to the subordinate side. As soon as you see the ball appearing over your shoulder, throw the ball in your subordinate hand. With practice you will be able to throw successive dominant-hand balls up and over the opposite shoulder, and then you can keep looking to that side.

OVER THE SHOULDER

In this variation, the ball is thrown over the shoulder on the same side as the hand that threw it; but apart from this, it is very similar to throwing behind your back. Practice with one, then two, balls before attempting to incorporate the variation into a three-ball pattern.

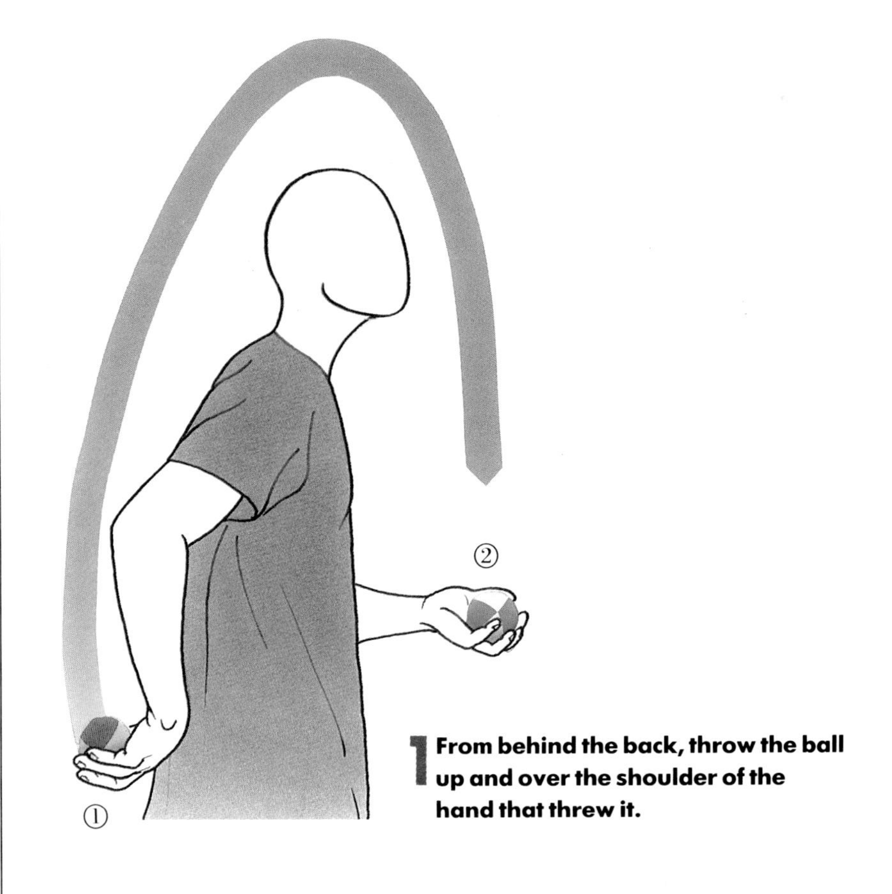

1 From behind the back, throw the ball up and over the shoulder of the hand that threw it.

2 As soon as the ball comes into view over your shoulder in front of you, throw the second ball from the same hand and begin to juggle in pattern.

Body Bounce Variations

For this group of variations you will need to use balls rather than beanbags. When you are learning these patterns, avoid solid rubber balls, which are both heavy and too bouncy – even if you do not hurt yourself, you will spend hours retrieving balls that have bounced away from you whenever you drop them.

You can bounce a ball off your forehead, knee, foot, forearm, elbow, or the back of your hand. Throw a ball at any of these points, bounce it, and catch it. Now, repeat the action, but as you catch the ball begin to juggle with it. Eventually you will be able to throw a ball at one of these points in the middle of a pattern, bounce it, and continue with the pattern as before.

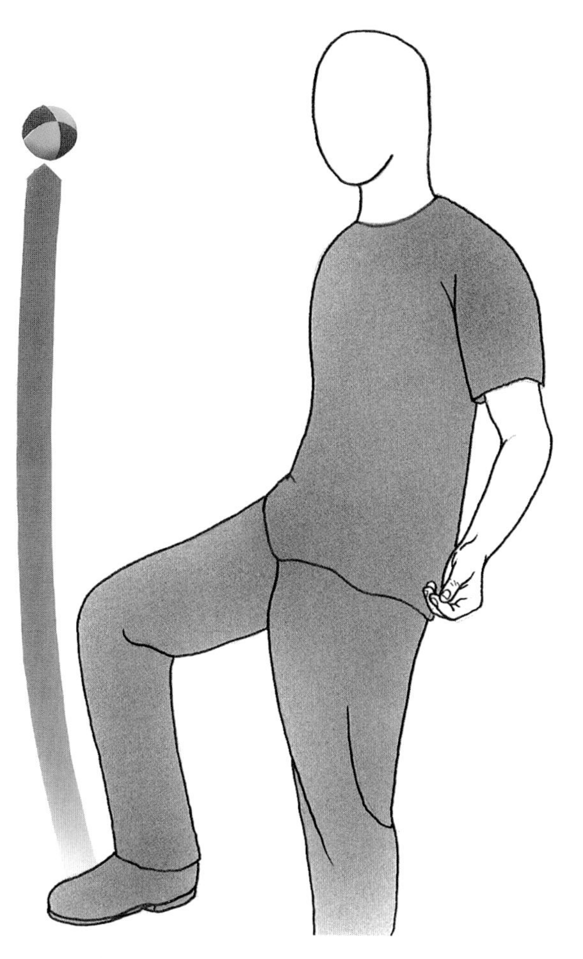

FOOT BOUNCE

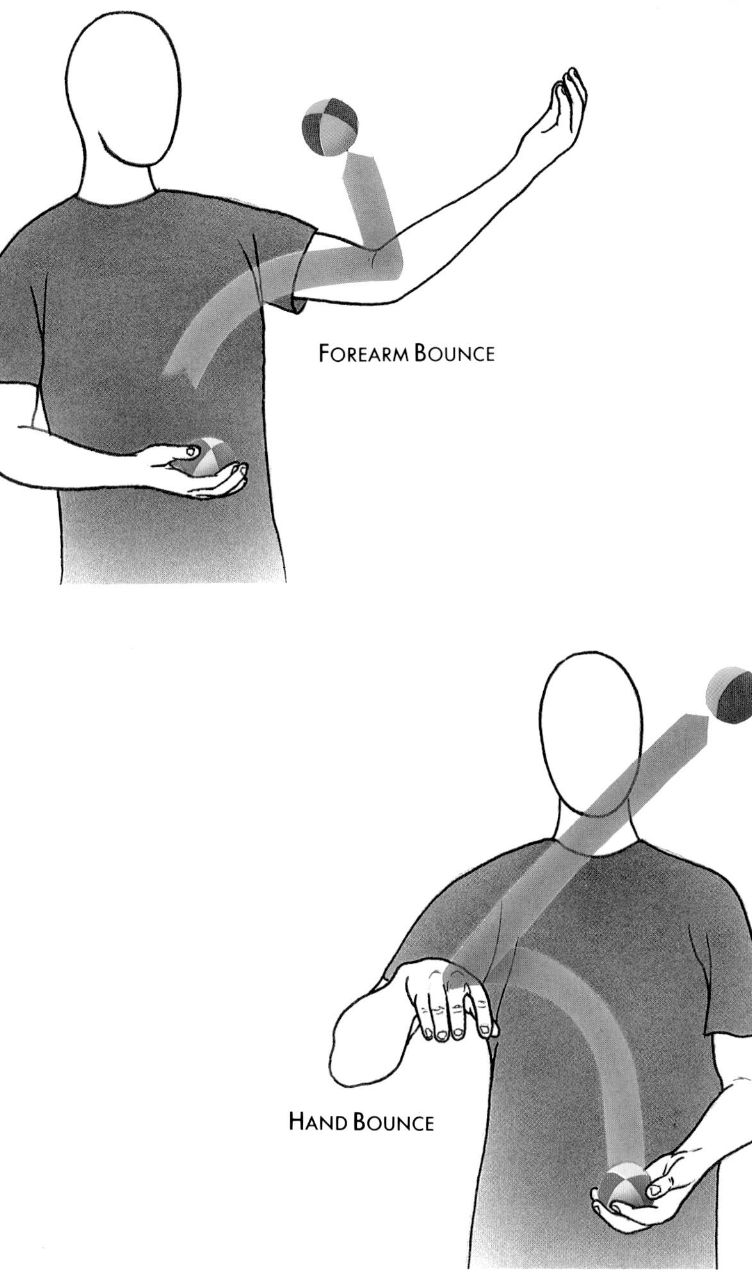

FOREARM BOUNCE

HAND BOUNCE

After practicing, you should be able to bounce a ball repeatedly from arm to arm or from knee to knee. The keys to successful body bounces are smaller and smaller bounces and lighter and lighter taps. Finesse is more important than force.

One of the most commonly seen tricks, even among non-jugglers, is when a ball is thrown by one hand and bounced off the same elbow. The secret of success is to bend the arm slightly and then straighten it at the moment of impact. You can incorporate this action into a juggling routine by throwing the ball a little higher than usual so that you have time to bend your elbow in readiness for the ball.

Bouncing a ball off a knee or thigh is comparatively easy, but regularly bouncing a ball from one thigh to another requires considerable practice. Other bounces that are difficult to master are those from a shoulder or onto a foot.

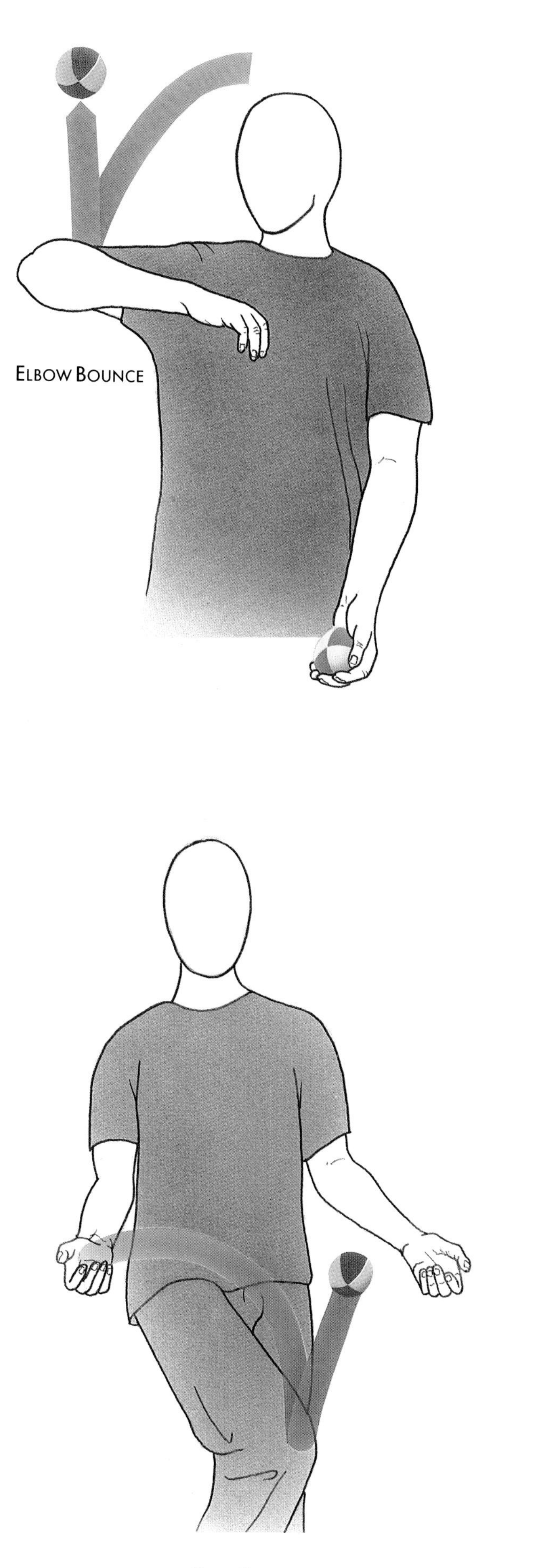

HEADING THE BALL

Before you begin this action, practice two separate movements.

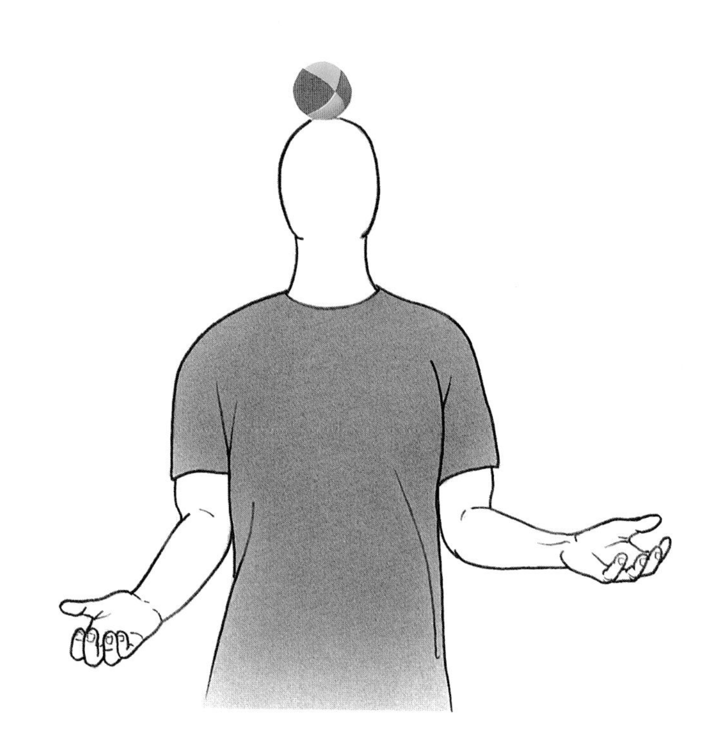

1. **Toss the ball high and catch it to give yourself an idea of how long it takes to fall the extra distance so that you can incorporate the movement into your pattern without disrupting your rhythm.**
2. **Take a ball and toss it from your dominant hand to your forehead and thence to your subordinate hand. Soccer players will find this easy, but remember that you must keep your eye on the ball. Try not to blink, or you will lose sight of the ball as it travels to your subordinate hand.**

When you practice, it is a good idea to count the number of times you can successfully head the ball without dropping it. Now that you have learned the height and bounce variations, the head bounce can be incorporated into a juggling pattern.

One of the most popular juggling routines with audiences is the continuous head bounce. You will have to move your head rapidly from side to side to head the ball each time it bounces.

Eating an Apple

Although this is one of the simplest tricks to learn, it is one that is often requested by audiences. First, wash a ball – this is going to be your "apple."

TIP

When you begin this trick, use one of the soft varieties of apple!

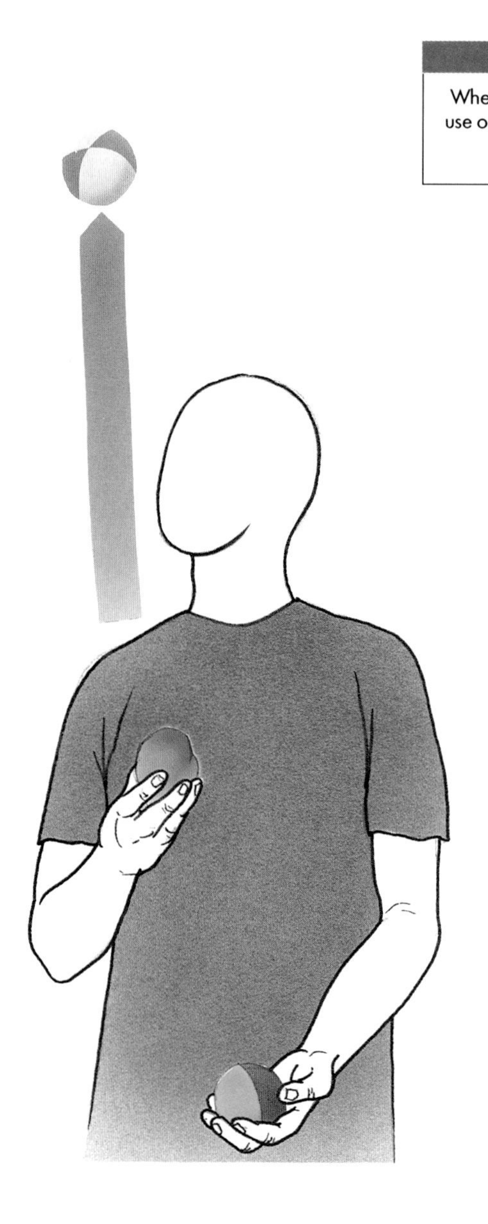

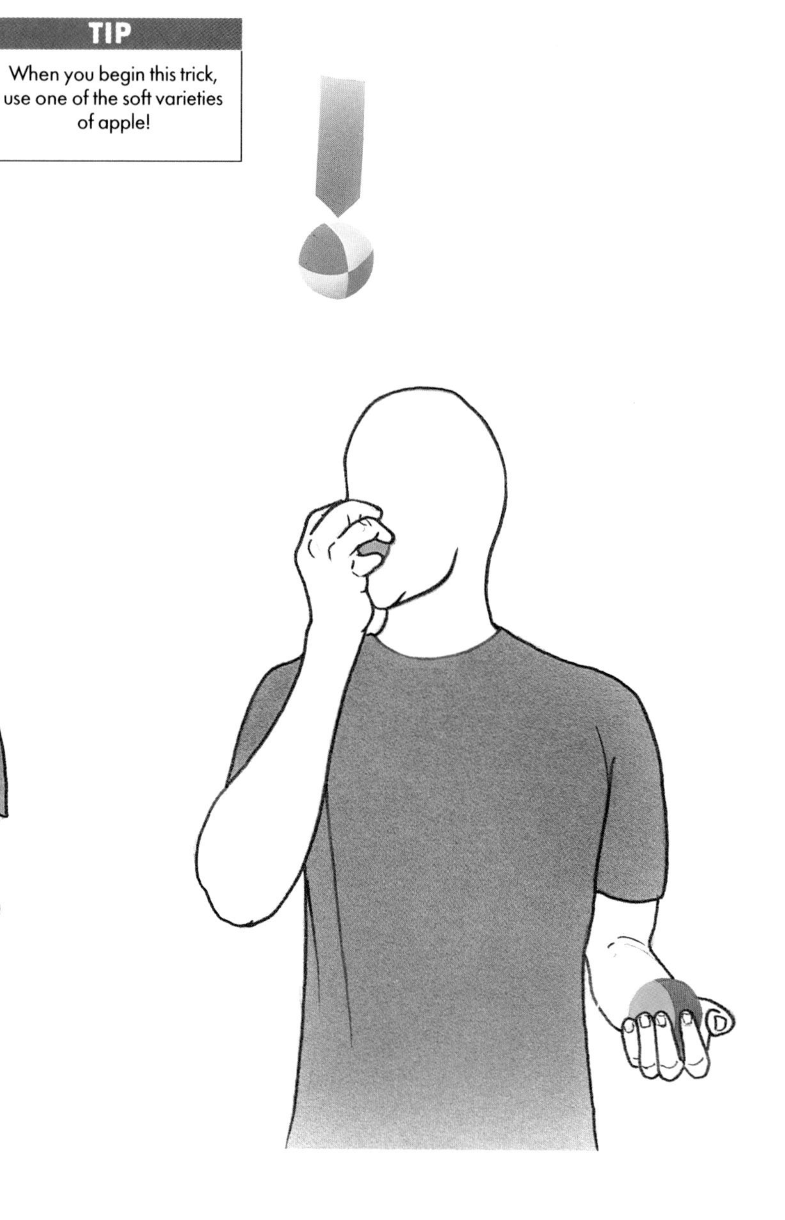

1 **Begin to juggle a cascade pattern. Every third time the "apple" comes into your dominant hand, throw the following ball (the one from your subordinate hand) higher than normal. The extra height will give you sufficient time to raise the "apple" to your lips and kiss it.**

2 **As soon as you have kissed the "apple," lower your hand and quickly throw the "apple" into the cascade pattern.**

As you practice this routine, gradually throw the following ball lower and lower until it is no higher than the normal cascade pattern. When you can kiss the "apple" on every pass, use a real apple and start to take bites. Begin with every third pass of the apple, then every second pass, and finally bite it every time it comes to your dominant hand.

Flashy Starts

By the time you have worked your way through this much of the book, you should have a good repertoire of your own ways of beginning a routine. These two starting patterns are very useful, however, and are well worth learning.

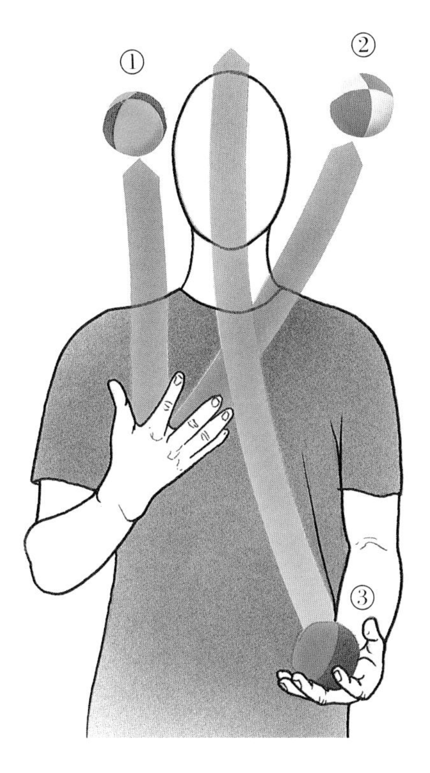

1 Throw both balls from your dominant hand into the air at the same time so that they separate as they rise. Throw the third ball from your subordinate hand so that it goes up between the other two balls.

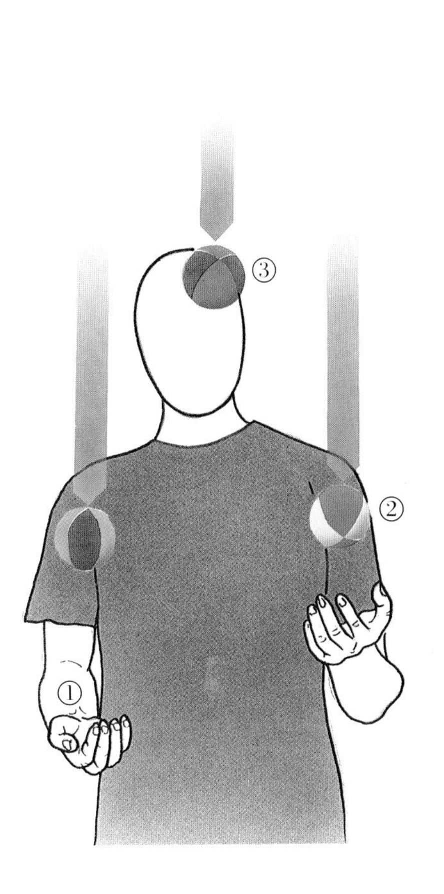

2 Catch the first two balls, one in each hand, and go straight into a cascade pattern.

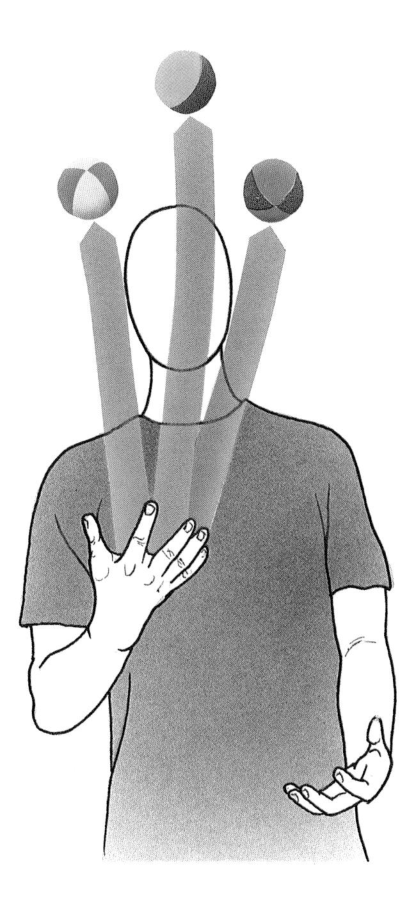

1 Hold three balls in your dominant hand. You will need to have two balls side by side in your palm, held in place by your thumb and little finger, while the third ball is held forward of the other two and held by your fingers only. When you throw the balls into the air, the ball in front will travel farther than the other two and will, therefore, be the last to be caught.

The two balls should rise parallel to each other, and you should raise one of your hands to snatch the outside ball – for example, if your right hand is dominant, raise your right hand and snatch the right-hand ball. Scoop the ball outward and up as the first throw in a cascade pattern. Your left hand will catch the left-hand ball and throw it up into the pattern, while the third ball should be caught in the usual way by the right hand so that you can continue the cascade pattern as normal.

Pauses

A pause can be an important part of a juggling routine, especially in the middle of a fast and furious act. It will come as a shock and a surprise. The pause is created by catching a ball with a part of your body other than your hand, pausing, then resuming the movement by flicking the ball back into the pattern. The most popular places to catch a ball are in the elbow, on the back of the neck, on the foot, and on the back of the hand.

Neck

You should practice catching the ball on the back of your neck with only one ball to begin with. You must hold the ball directly in front of yourself and toss it back at right angles to your body, just as if you were going to head the ball. When the ball is about 6 inches from your head, raise your shoulders and stretch your neck to make a pocket in which to catch the ball. As you do this, slowly lower your torso and gently bend your knees so that the ball sits snugly in the back of your neck. Both arms will be held in inverted Vs.

When you want to flick the ball back into the juggling pattern, nod your head forward and bring it sharply back. The ball will roll forward as you bring your head down and will be jerked into the air.

To achieve this movement successfully when you are juggling, you must make sure that the balls are moving smoothly and that the ball to be caught on your neck is not thrown too high.

Elbow

When you want to catch a ball in your elbow, you will have to give the balls a little extra height to give yourself time. If you are going to catch the ball in your left elbow, throw the ball from your right hand a little higher. Raise your left elbow to meet the ball and move it down slightly more slowly than the speed at which the ball is traveling. The ball will rest gently in the crook of your elbow until you are ready to flick it up into the pattern again.

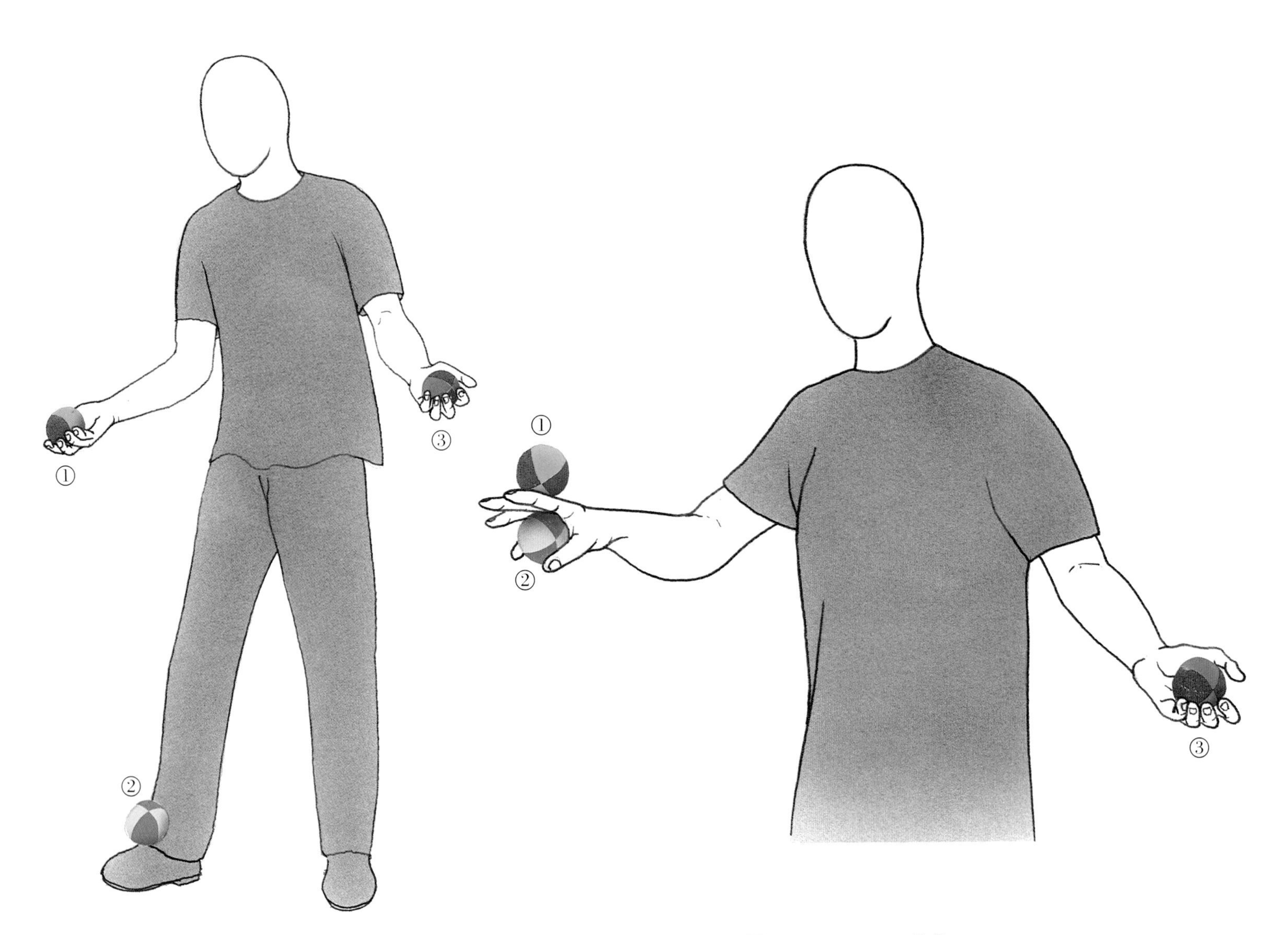

FOOT

Raise your toe slightly and absorb the shock of the ball with your knee as it lands.

BACK OF HAND

Catch the ball at the highest point of its trajectory by inserting your hand under it.

Recoveries

As you will by now have discovered, dropping a ball is a fairly regular event. However, it is possible to turn a dropped ball into part of your routine – watch professional jugglers to see how often it happens.

One of the easiest ways is to roll the dropped ball with one foot onto the toe of the other foot. Alternatively, bend down quickly, pick up the errant ball, and toss it up extra high. Wait for it to come down – you could do a bit of "business" while you wait, such as whistling or shielding your eyes – and return it to your juggling pattern.

Alternatively, drop the other two balls, one on each side of the dropped ball, and do a "shell game" with them on the ground, hopping one over the other for a while in a cascade pattern, before picking them all up and beginning again.

THREE-BALL BOUNCE JUGGLING

Instead of juggling upward, try juggling downward by bouncing the balls. If this is your first attempt at juggling with props other than the standard juggling balls or beanbags – or even rings and clubs – you will find that knowing the basic patterns, especially the cascade (which you should be able to do in your sleep by now), will enable you to concentrate on the technique required for the balls you are juggling.

Equipment

You need a smooth, flat floor and very bouncy balls.

If you do not have a suitable floor, you could use a sheet of thin wooden board or a marble slab. The area need not be large. At first you may find that you spend a good deal of time recovering balls that have bounced away, and if this is the case, you might want to create a high-sided surround to trap the wild balls.

The best balls to use are the specially made silicon juggling balls, but they are quite expensive. Good alternatives are lacrosse balls or dog balls. Ordinary tennis balls will do just as well, although they will not bounce as high as the silicon balls.

Floor Bounce Techniques

There are two types of bounce – the forced and non-forced.

NON-FORCED

In non-forced bouncing, which is generally used for five balls or more, the balls are gently tossed so that they bounce in small arcs up to your hands. This is easier than forced bouncing.

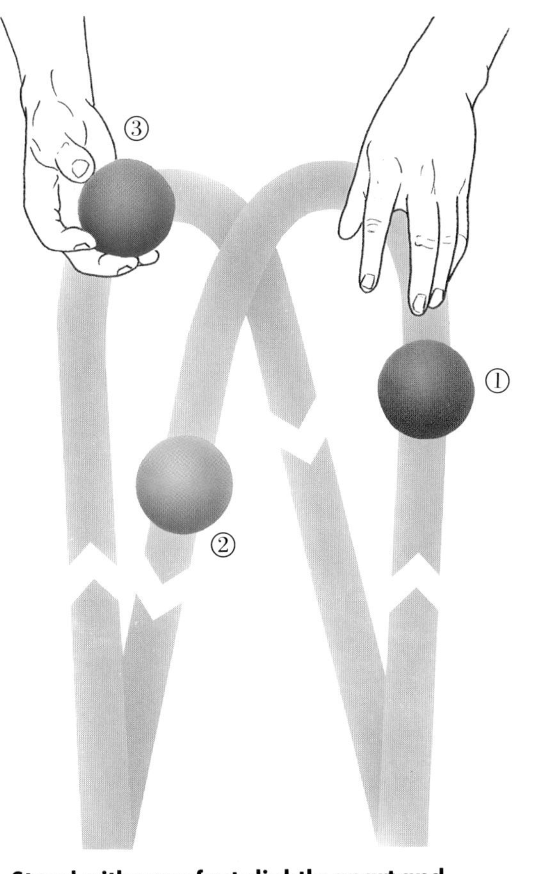

1 Stand with your feet slightly apart and your weight evenly balanced. With your palms up, toss the balls gently upward and allow them to bounce on the floor. Catch the balls with your palms down.

REMEMBER

- **There are two bounce points.**
- **The balls cross on the way down.**
- **The balls travel downward on the inside and return on the outside.**

FORCED

In forced bouncing, you throw the balls downward, and they rise as high as or higher than the release point. This method is most often used with three-ball bouncing.

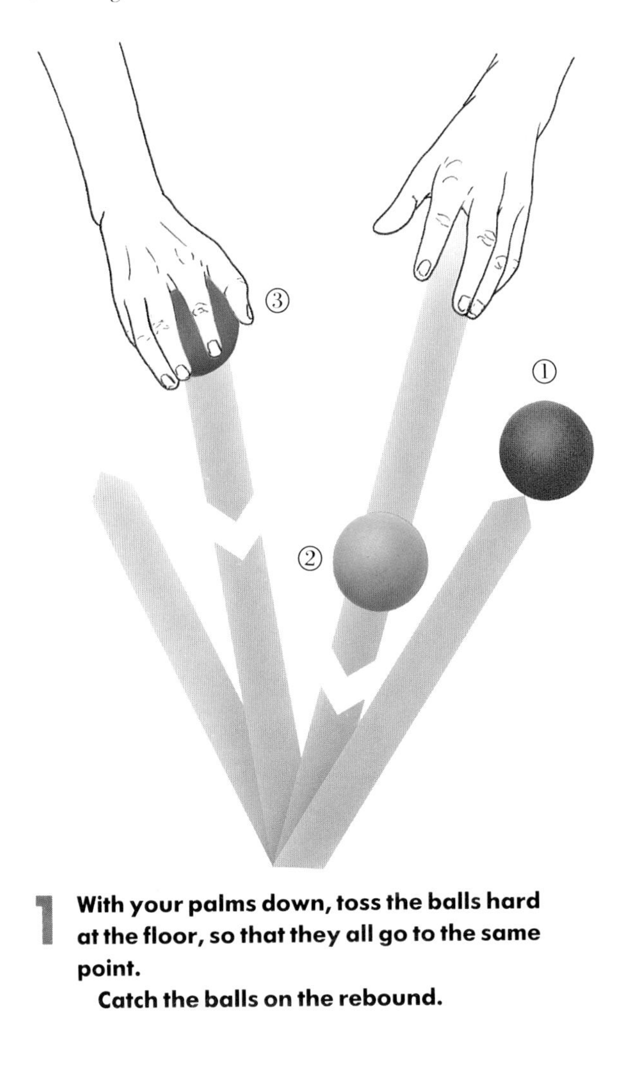

1 With your palms down, toss the balls hard at the floor, so that they all go to the same point.

Catch the balls on the rebound.

REMEMBER

- **There is one bounce point.**
- **The balls should always be caught on the rebound.**

Floor Bounce Variations

When you have practiced bouncing the balls and have gotten used to the timing, try throwing them, using the non-forced technique, in a reverse-cascade pattern.

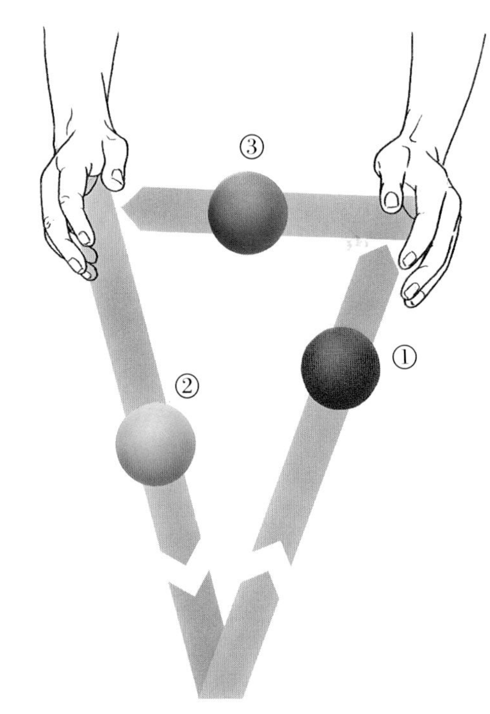

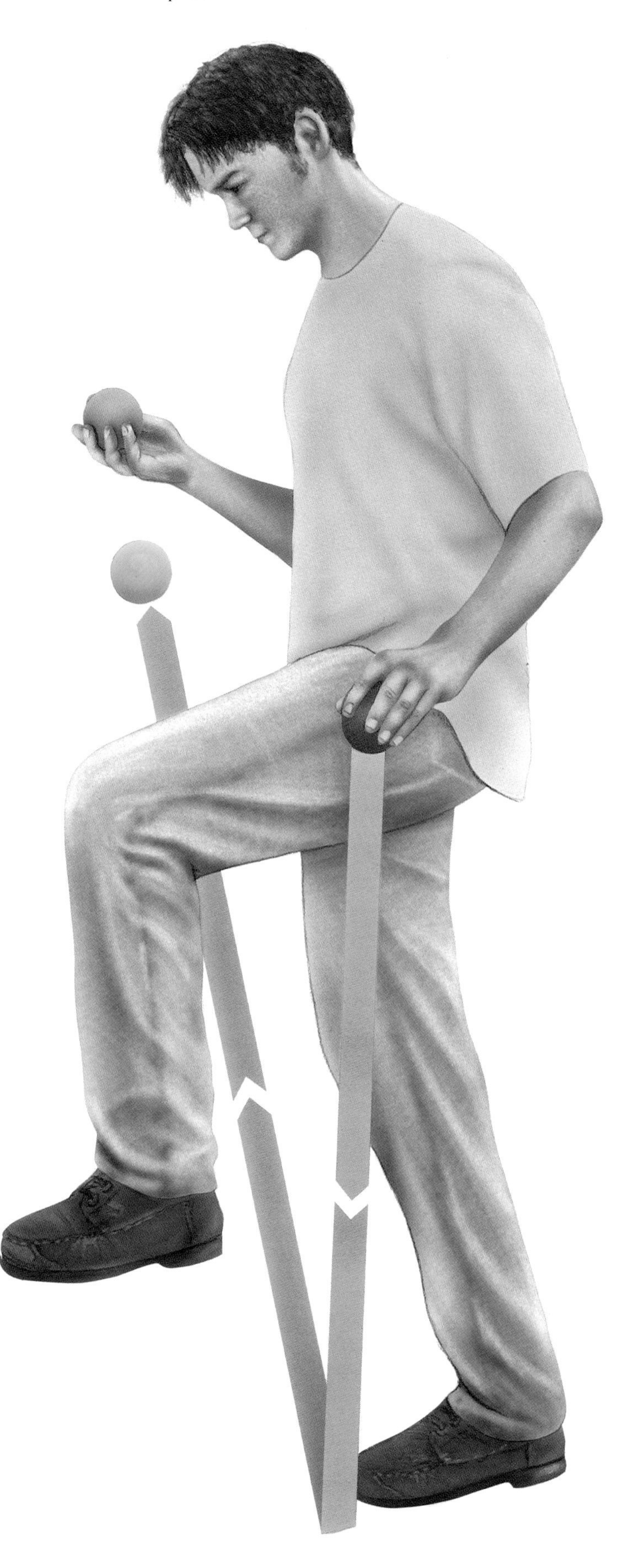

1 Begin with two balls in your dominant hand and one in your subordinate hand, and let the balls from your dominant hand hit the floor at a point just in front of your opposite foot. The ball from your subordinate hand should hit a point just in front of the other foot.

You should use the forced technique for the basic shower pattern. Here, there will be only one bounce point, mid-way between your feet.

One of the most popular variations is to raise your knee as you bounce juggle so that one ball goes under your leg. Practice until you can do this with either leg. You will then be able to build a routine in which you can bounce the balls under each leg alternately.

The other obvious variation is to mix bounce juggling with normal three-ball juggling. You will, of course, need to use bouncy balls – not beanbags.

Although this chapter has looked at three-ball bounce juggling only, as with ordinary ball juggling you can, once you have mastered the basic techniques, go on to bounce juggling with five balls. The principles are exactly the same, although you should use the non-forced technique. Even with three-ball bounce juggling, however, the scope for developing your own variations is virtually unlimited, and there are great opportunities for experimentation.

MORE ADVANCED BALL JUGGLING

Once they have mastered juggling with three balls, many jugglers become obsessed with the idea of juggling with four or even five balls. If you are determined to achieve this, you must be ready to put in long hours of practice.

Juggling with Four Balls

Columns

The simplest four-ball pattern is to juggle with two balls in each hand so that the balls thrown from each hand travel on parallel paths. Practice with each hand separately before trying four balls.

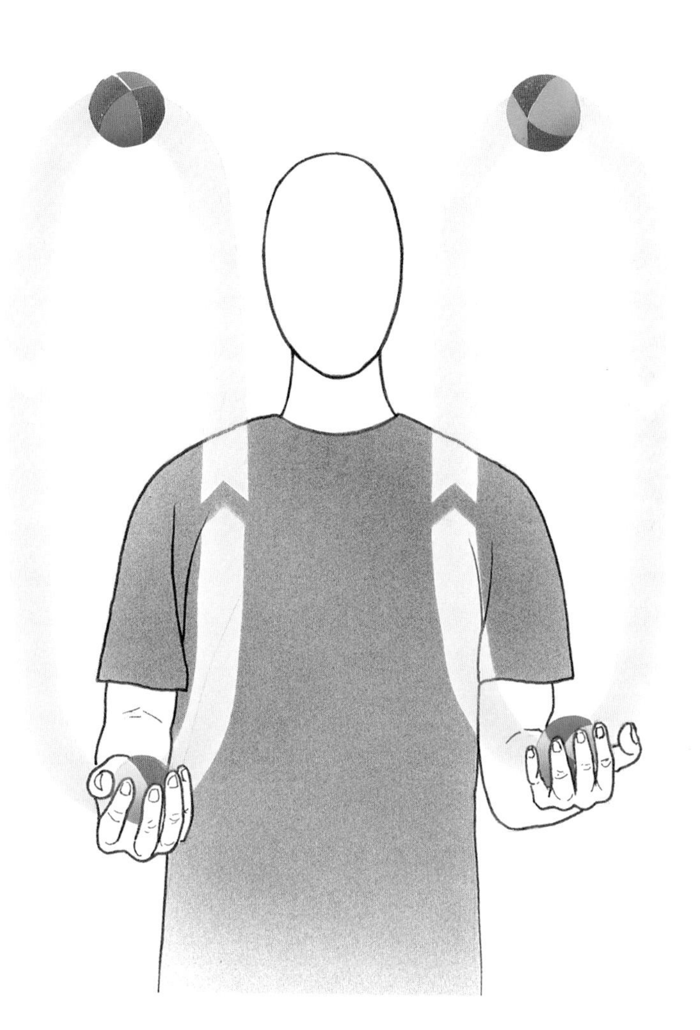

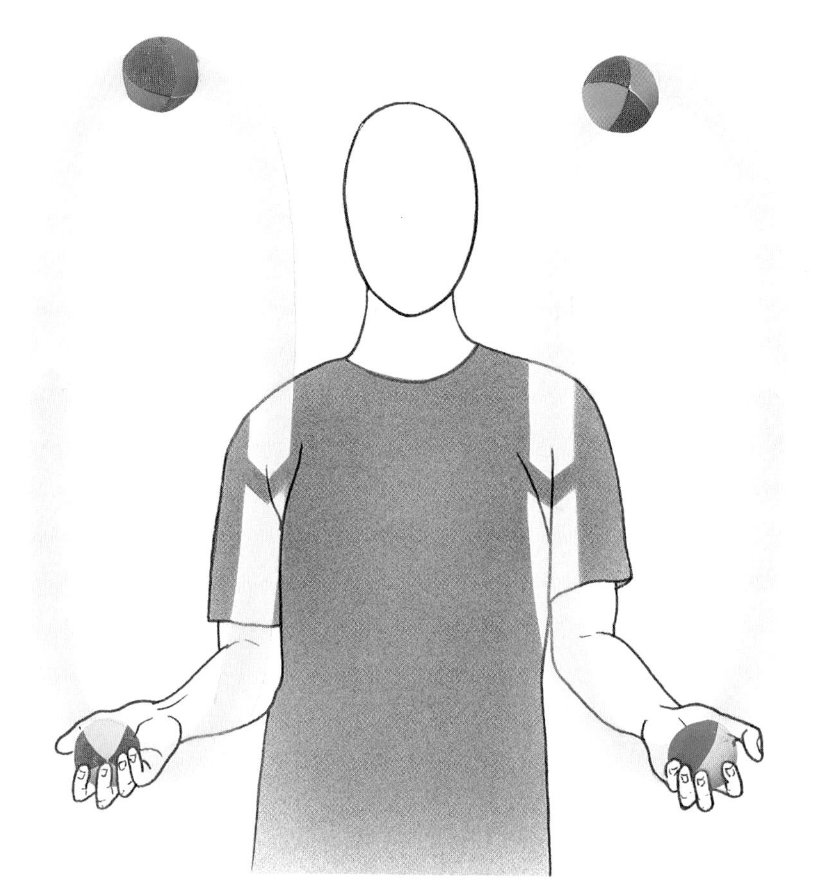

1 **First, juggle so that each hand makes an inward scoop, as in the basic three-ball columns (see Chapter 1). Catch on the outside, scoop toward the inside (that is, toward the midline of your body), and throw. Every time a ball reaches the peak of its trajectory, throw the next ball.**

TIP

To begin with, collisions and crossed balls are inevitable. Use two balls of the same color in your dominant hand and two balls of a different color in your subordinate hand. Don't let the colors change hands.

2 **Next, try the outward scoop, in which you catch on the inside (the midline of your body), scoop toward the outside, and throw.**

When you have established a smooth rhythm, you could try introducing a few variations. You could mix the outward and inward scoops so that one hand is throwing with an inward scoop and your other hand is using an outward scoop. This is actually quite hard to do but does look very effective – just remember that the balls should never cross the midline. You could also experiment by introducing extra high throws, juggling each hand at a different tempo, or moving around while you juggle.

Shower

It is possible to juggle the shower pattern with four balls, but most people find that it is more difficult than four-ball columns.

1 **Start with three balls in your dominant hand and one in your subordinate hand.**

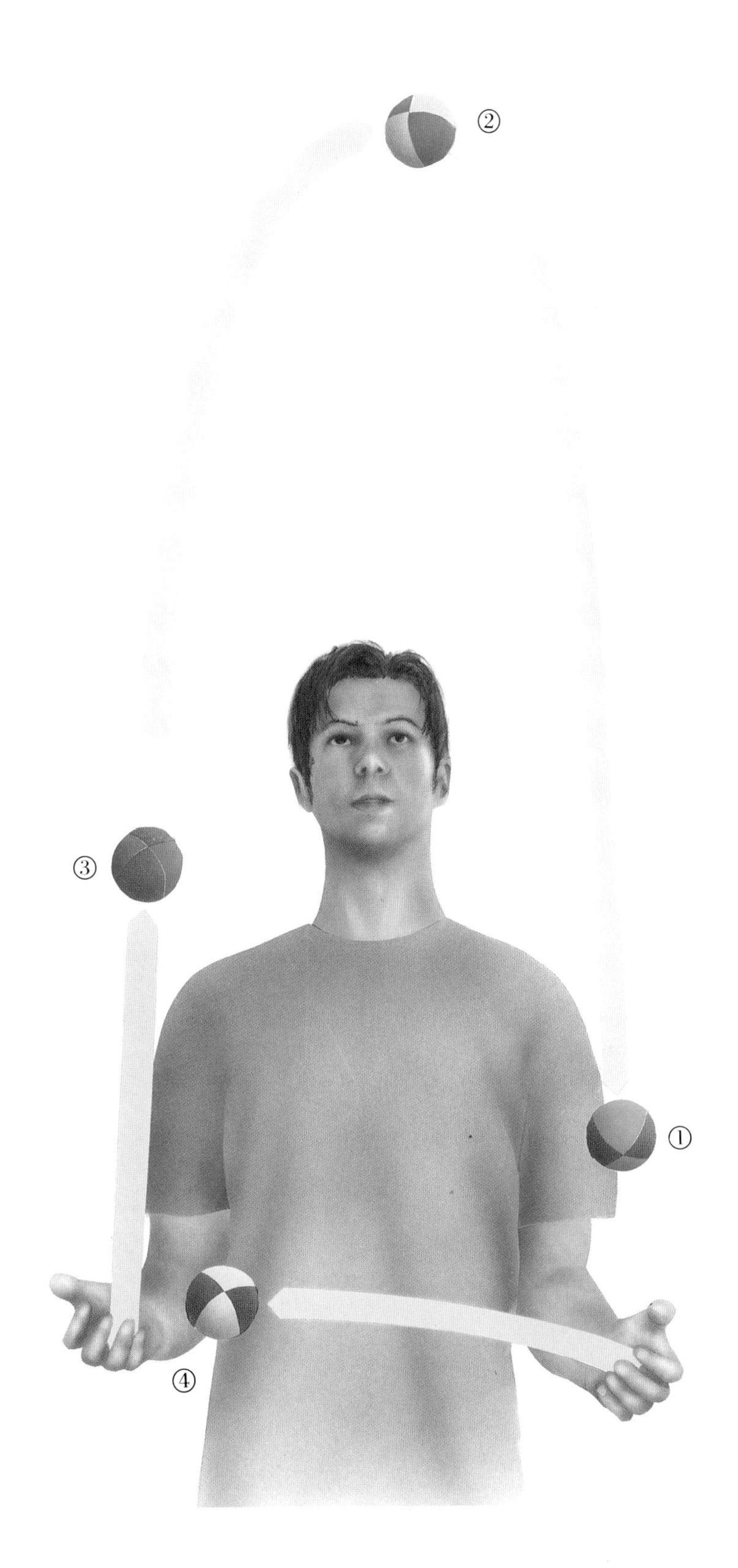

2 **Throw the first three balls in rapid succession; you must throw them quite high.**

3 **Just before the first ball lands, pass the fourth ball to your empty, dominant hand and throw it.**

Juggling with Five Balls

For many people, juggling with five balls represents the height of their ambition. Some people find it very difficult to master, while others find it relatively easy.

You may wish to use five differently colored balls, and you will probably find it helpful for following these patterns if you actually write the numbers 1–5 on them.

CASCADE

The five-ball cascade pattern is the same as the three-ball cascade except that three balls are always in the air at the same time. You will also have to throw the balls higher than usual. Try the following way of building up to the five-ball cascade. You may have to repeat each individual step several times before you are ready to move on to the next one.

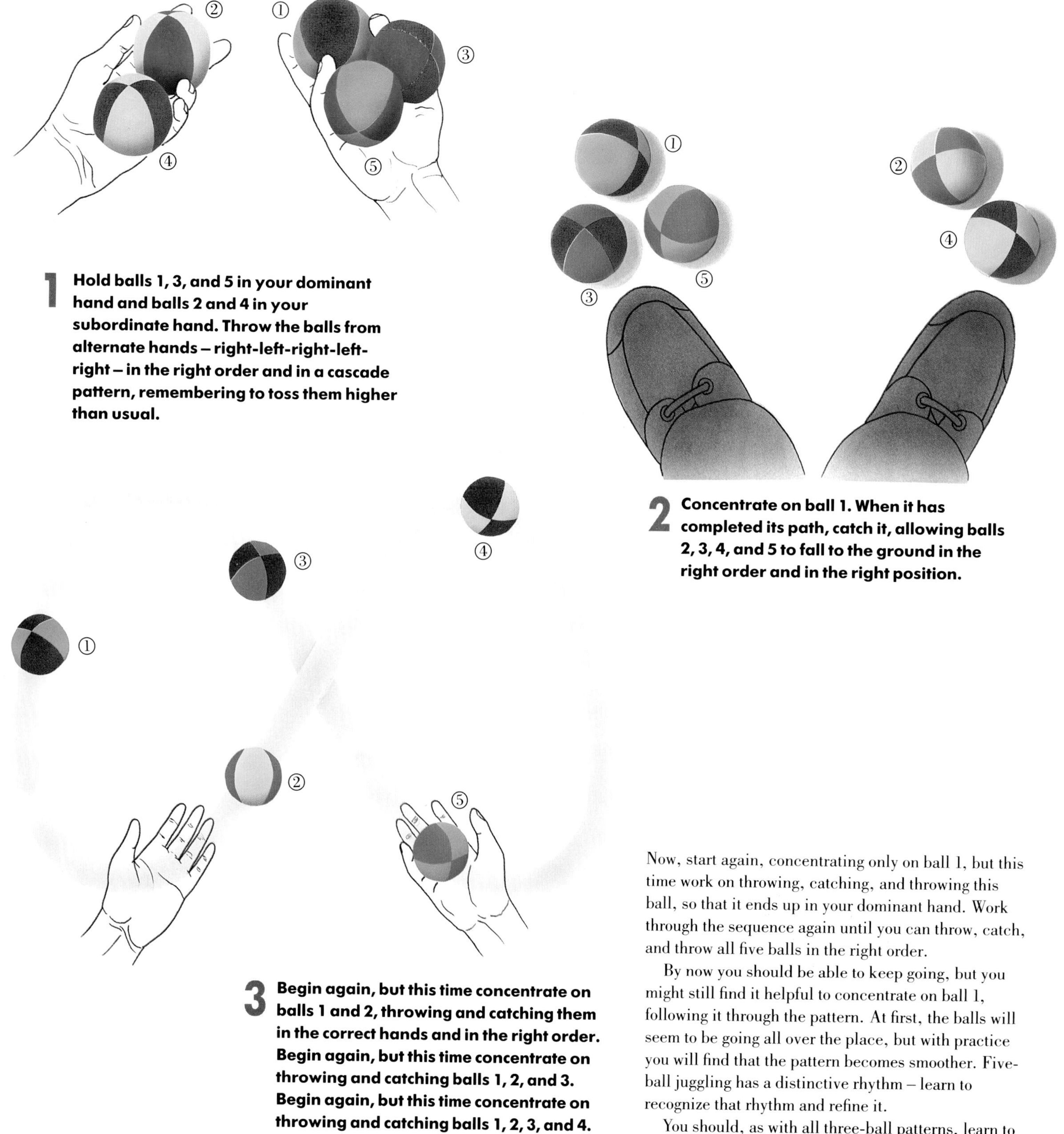

1 **Hold balls 1, 3, and 5 in your dominant hand and balls 2 and 4 in your subordinate hand. Throw the balls from alternate hands – right-left-right-left-right – in the right order and in a cascade pattern, remembering to toss them higher than usual.**

2 **Concentrate on ball 1. When it has completed its path, catch it, allowing balls 2, 3, 4, and 5 to fall to the ground in the right order and in the right position.**

3 **Begin again, but this time concentrate on balls 1 and 2, throwing and catching them in the correct hands and in the right order. Begin again, but this time concentrate on throwing and catching balls 1, 2, and 3. Begin again, but this time concentrate on throwing and catching balls 1, 2, 3, and 4. Then, throw and catch all five balls in the correct order.**

Now, start again, concentrating only on ball 1, but this time work on throwing, catching, and throwing this ball, so that it ends up in your dominant hand. Work through the sequence again until you can throw, catch, and throw all five balls in the right order.

By now you should be able to keep going, but you might still find it helpful to concentrate on ball 1, following it through the pattern. At first, the balls will seem to be going all over the place, but with practice you will find that the pattern becomes smoother. Five-ball juggling has a distinctive rhythm – learn to recognize that rhythm and refine it.

You should, as with all three-ball patterns, learn to juggle five-ball patterns with both your subordinate and dominant hand.

Five-ball Variations

When you have succeeded in getting five balls into the air in a regular, smooth pattern, you may feel confident enough to introduce a movement such as throwing a ball under your leg. You may even feel you want to increase the number of balls to seven . . . or nine. Most of the three-ball variations (see Chapter 2) can be juggled with five balls, including the body shots. The most popular variations, however, are the half-shower, the reverse-cascade, juggler's tennis, and the shower.

HALF-SHOWER

1 Begin with three balls in your dominant hand and two in your subordinate hand. Make the first five throws quickly – "Right-left-right-left-right" – and as soon as you catch a ball, throw it along its path.

Now, make sure that you can perform a five-ball half-shower beginning with three balls in your subordinate hand.

① ② ③ ④ ⑤

REVERSE-CASCADE

As soon as you can perform a five-ball half-shower beginning with your subordinate hand and dominant hand equally easily, the reverse-cascade is relatively simple to learn.

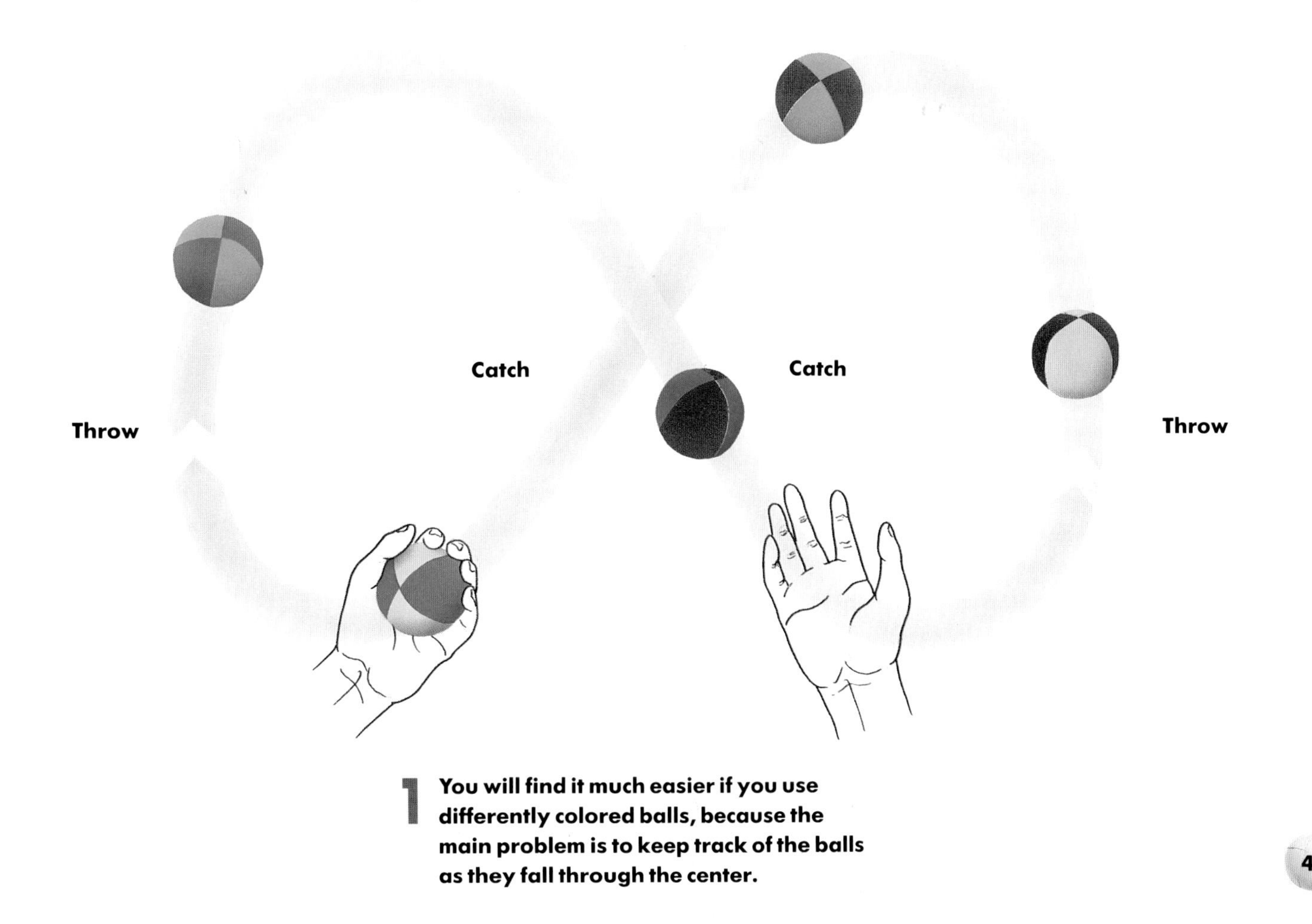

1 You will find it much easier if you use differently colored balls, because the main problem is to keep track of the balls as they fall through the center.

JUGGLER'S TENNIS

Being able to juggle a five-ball half-shower with both hands will enable you to do juggler's tennis with five balls.

1 **Begin juggling a five-ball cascade, then toss one ball to and fro over the top.**

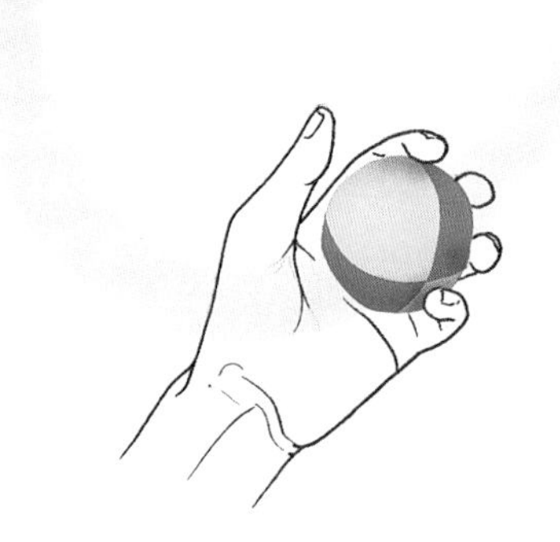

TIP

It will take you a long time to get used to working with five balls. You might find it helpful to practice the three-ball flash (see Chapter 2). In this movement, all three balls are in the air at the same time while you clap your hands. When you progress to five balls, the clap is replaced by the two additional balls.

SHOWER

1 **Begin with only four balls and take them all in your dominant hand. Throw all four balls rapidly along the same path and catch them in your subordinate hand – "Throw-throw-throw-throw-catch-catch-catch-catch."**

2 **Next, try to repeat the move, but each time you catch a ball in your subordinate hand, pass it quickly to your dominant hand and throw it again.**

3 **Now, start with four balls in your dominant hand and one in your subordinate hand. As soon as you have tossed the first four balls, pass the ball from your subordinate hand to your dominant hand. Continue the routine by throwing every ball that comes to your dominant hand and passing every ball that comes to your subordinate hand.**

THREE-BALL JUGGLING PATTERNS FOR TWO PEOPLE

Most people take up juggling because they have a friend who juggles or because they accompany a friend to a juggling workshop. However you became interested in juggling, you will find that three-ball patterns with two people will be a logical extension of your new skill and will also add extra enjoyment to your hobby. At first, working with another person will require patience – but remember that you will probably drop the balls as often as your partner does. There are dozens of possible patterns and variations. Those described in this chapter are the most basic and the easiest to learn, but as you and your partner become more experienced, you will probably want to develop your own movements and build more complicated routines.

Three-ball Stealing from the Front

Stand in front of your partner. The aim is for juggler 1 to begin to juggle a cascade pattern and for juggler 2 to reach out and take the balls, continuing to juggle a cascade pattern without breaking the rhythm.

It is essential that both you and your partner have the same dominant and subordinate hands – that is, you must both lead either with your right hand or with your left hand.

Although the patterns and moves described here use balls, most of them can also be done with clubs (see Chapter 9).

1 Stand close to your partner, face to face, so that you can share the juggling space. Use three differently colored balls.

Begin to juggle a three-ball cascade pattern, fairly slowly and keeping your hands low but tossing the balls a little higher than usual.

Your partner should select one of the balls and, when you throw that ball from your dominant to your subordinate hand, he/she should take the ball as it reaches its peak with his/her dominant hand.

2 Immediately after taking the first ball, your partner should take the next ball at its peak with his/her subordinate hand as you throw it from your subordinate to your dominant hand.

3 Your partner now has one ball in each hand. Maintaining your rhythm, throw the third ball from your dominant to your subordinate hand. As this ball peaks, your partner should throw the first ball into a cascade pattern and catch the third ball with his/her dominant hand, maintaining the rhythm you have established.

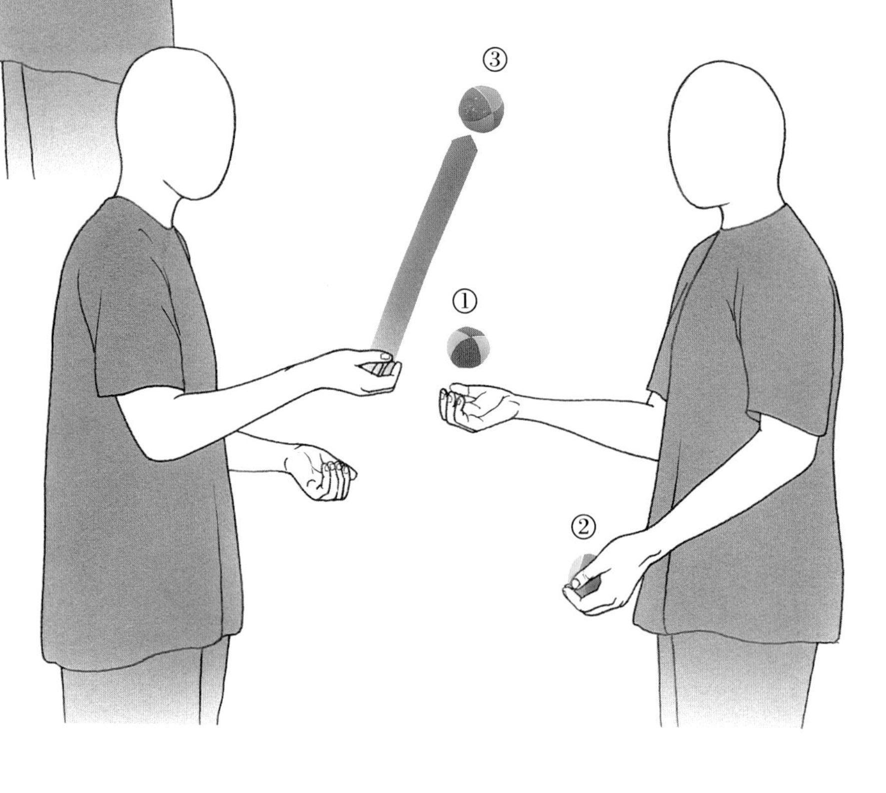

Your partner can continue to juggle for a while, or you can "steal" the balls back on the next throw.

If the movement is going to look effective, it is important that juggler 2 does appear to "steal" the balls, rather than just having them passed along by juggler 1.

Three-ball Stealing from the Side

This is similar to three-ball stealing from the front, but the aim is to make it appear that juggler 1 loses the balls before he/she is aware that juggler 2 is there. Juggler 2 should approach juggler 1 from behind and a little to one side so that he/she can slide his/her dominant hand between juggler 1's forearms and the balls.

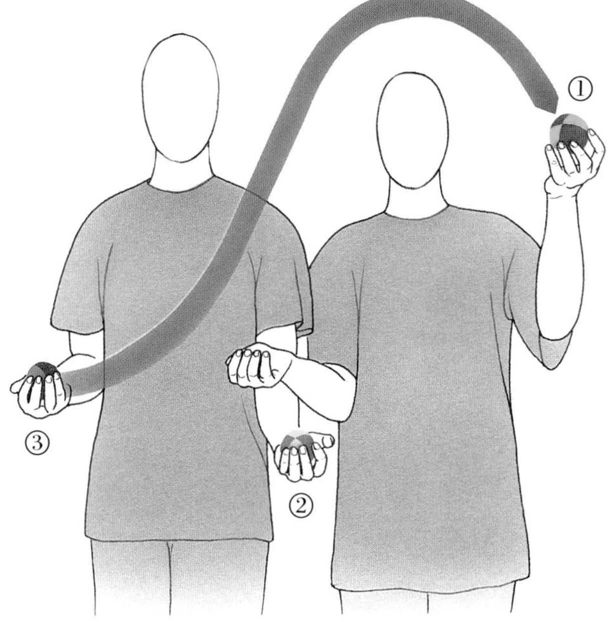

1 **Begin to juggle a three-ball cascade pattern. Your partner should adopt a position from which he/she can take a ball destined for your subordinate hand with his/her subordinate hand. Your partner must reach up high to take the ball at its peak.**

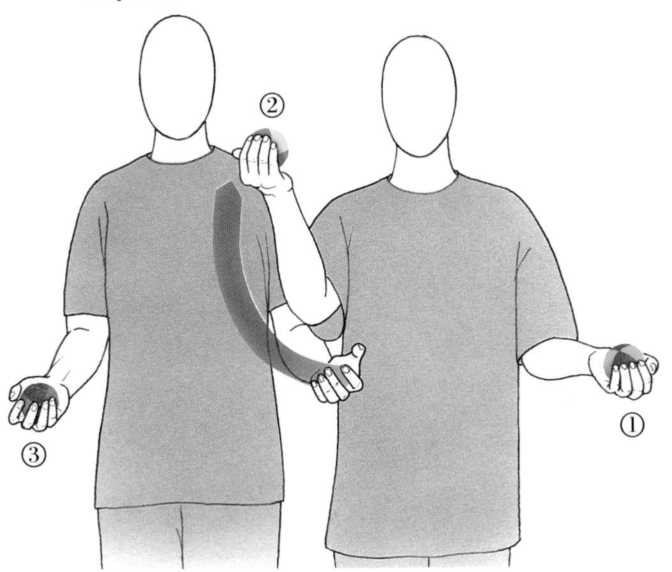

2 **As soon as your partner has the ball in his/her subordinate hand, he/she should reach across in front of you to take the next ball, the one intended for your dominant hand, with his/her dominant hand.**

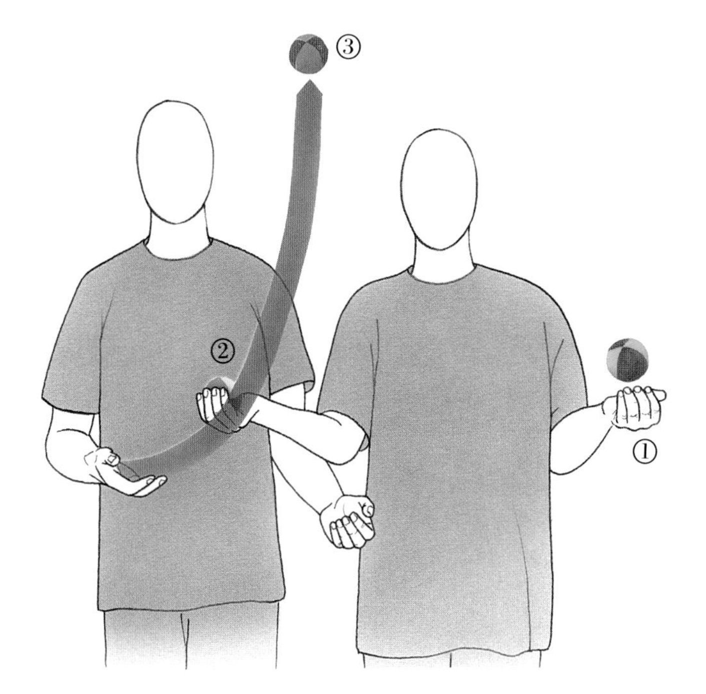

3 **Now that your partner has a ball in each hand, you should throw the third ball on its normal path toward your subordinate hand.**

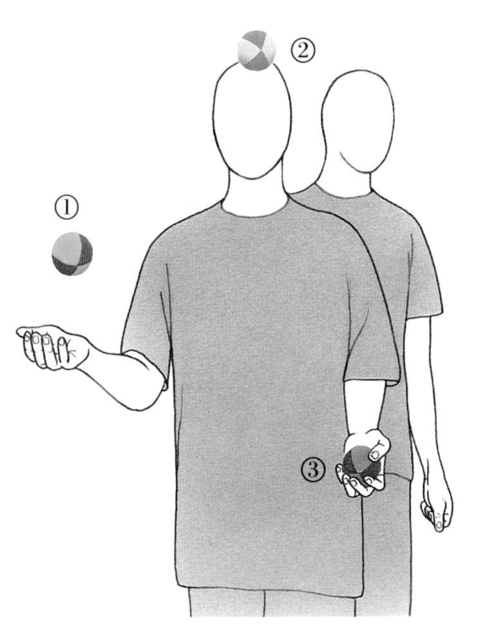

4 **As soon as this third ball reaches the peak of its trajectory, you should step slightly away from your partner and slightly back. Your partner should step into your position, throw a ball from his/her subordinate hand, take the third ball in that hand, and continue to juggle a cascade pattern without disrupting the rhythm you established.**

The aim should be for both you and your partner to move around and behind each other, from side to side, sharing the three balls in a continuous movement.

Audiences thoroughly enjoy this routine, which is at its best when it begins slowly and builds to a frantic pace, with the jugglers moving around each other so quickly that the balls appear to remain in the same place while the jugglers rush around in circles.

Six-ball Juggling with a Partner

Now that you can share three balls with a partner, you can begin to think about juggling with six balls, passing the balls between you. Before you begin to attempt this, however, you must both be able to juggle a smooth, rhythmic cascade pattern.

PASSING THE BALLS

BEGINNING TO JUGGLE

It is worth taking some time and trouble working on beginning your juggling sequence at exactly the same time. The standard way of starting is for each of you to hold two balls in your dominant hand, and one ball in your subordinate hand. Stand face to face with your partner. One of you should raise both hands to shoulder level; your partner should do the same. Then you both bring your hands down at the same moment, and begin to juggle. If you do not synchronize your first throw, the whole sequence will fail. Practice this opening movement time and again, until you both throw the first ball at precisely the same moment.

ESTABLISHING A RHYTHM

When you have learnt how to begin together, the next stage is to learn to juggle with the same rhythm. One of the best ways is for you both to count out loud as you throw the balls until you are both automatically throwing and catching at the same pace.

LEARNING TO PASS

After beginning together and juggling in unison, the next most important stage is to learn to pass at the same time. Most jugglers start off by passing the third ball to leave their dominant hands.

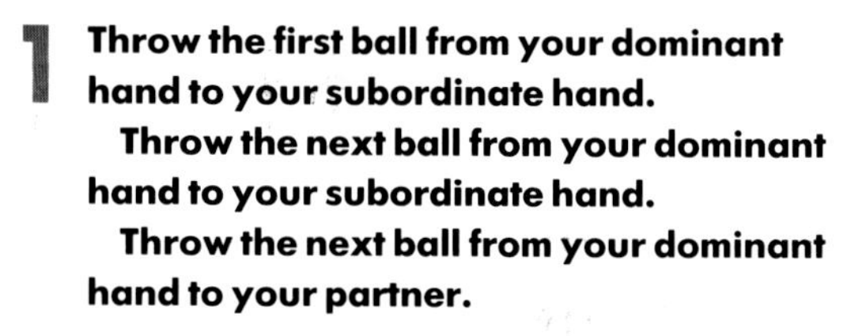

1 Throw the first ball from your dominant hand to your subordinate hand.
Throw the next ball from your dominant hand to your subordinate hand.
Throw the next ball from your dominant hand to your partner.

At first, before you gain experience of passing, you should practice passing with your partner with a pattern called **running three**, which uses three balls only.

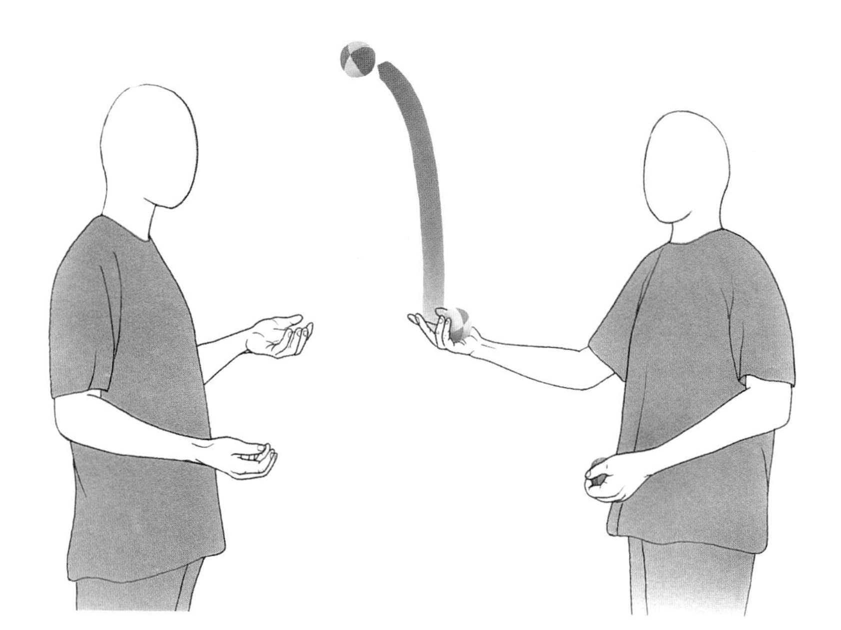

1 Stand about 6 ft. away from your partner.
Hold two balls in your dominant hand and one in your subordinate hand. Your partner holds none.
Begin juggling a three-ball cascade pattern, but throw one of your dominant hand balls toward your partner's subordinate hand.

Every throw from your dominant hand should go to your partner, while every throw from your subordinate hand goes across your chest to your dominant hand.

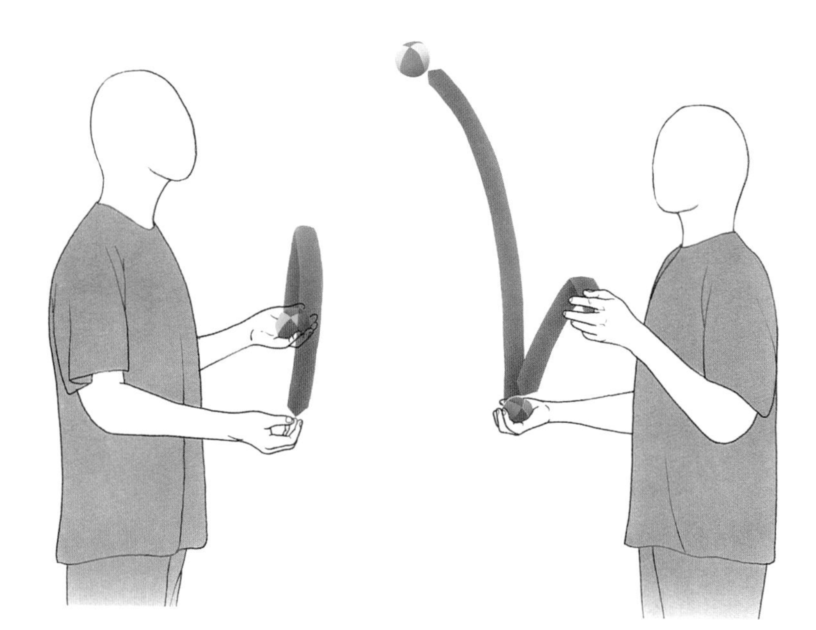

2 Your partner should catch each ball from your dominant hand in his/her subordinate hand, toss it across to his/her dominant hand, and begin to juggle so that when you throw across the third ball, your partner can settle into juggling a normal three-ball cascade.
Your partner should then return the balls to you in the same way.

Your aim is to pass the balls constantly so that they travel in a smooth, rectangular path between you and your partner.

When you both feel comfortable with the running three pattern, you can use six balls. The pattern is exactly the same, but you are both juggling with three balls but passing at the same time.

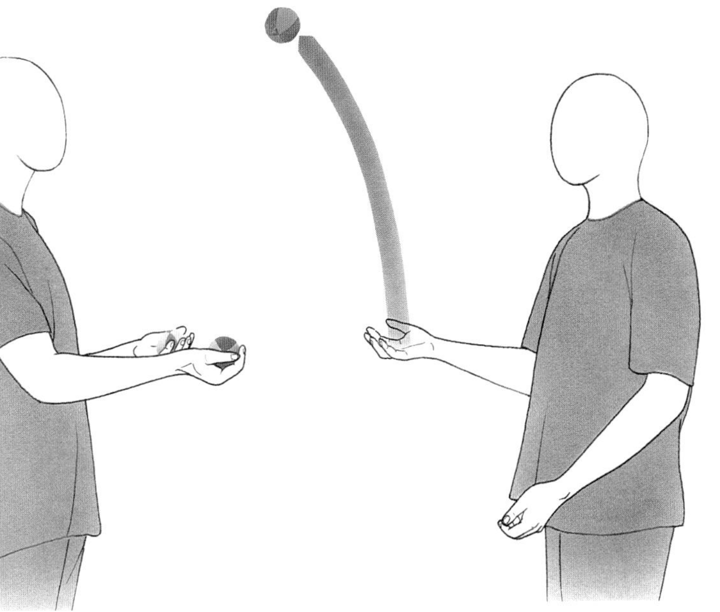

3 Both you and your partner begin to juggle a three-ball cascade.

At an agreed moment, both throw the ball in your dominant hands to your partner's subordinate hand.

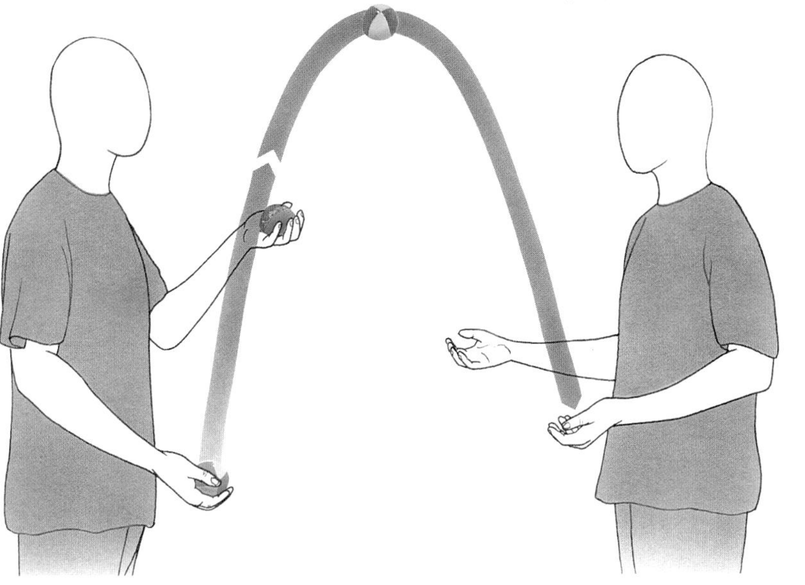

4 Establish a rhythm, with both counting each ball as it leaves your dominant hands – "two-one-pass, two-one-pass."

This routine is known as thirds, because you are passing every third ball from your dominant hands. However, whether you are passing the third, second, or every ball, it is usual to begin the routine by throwing the third ball to your partner.

As you become more practiced you may want to speed up the rate of passing by throwing every ball to your partner after the first three. Your rhythm will be "two-one-pass-pass-pass-pass," and this routine is known as passing solids or showering.

THREE-THREE-TEN

One of the most effective routines from the point of view of an audience is one that, by building up the rate at which passes are made, makes it appear that the throws themselves are being made twice as quickly. The routine is made up as follows:

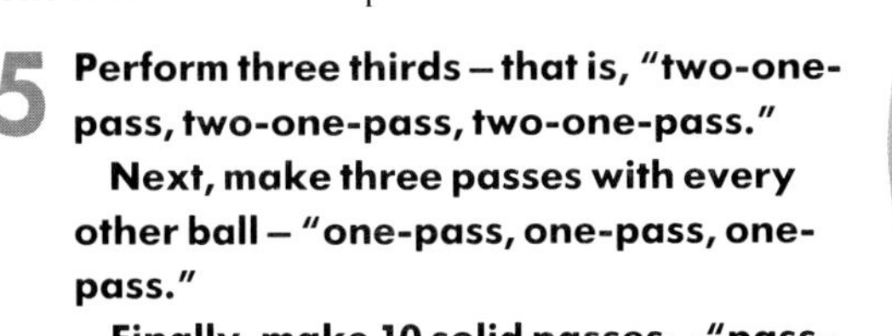

5 Perform three thirds – that is, "two-one-pass, two-one-pass, two-one-pass."

Next, make three passes with every other ball – "one-pass, one-pass, one-pass."

Finally, make 10 solid passes – "pass-pass-pass-pass-pass-pass-pass-pass-pass-pass-pass."

A neat way of finishing is to end on a dominant-hand throw – shout "halt" and throw the last ball extra high so that you both catch and finish at the same time.

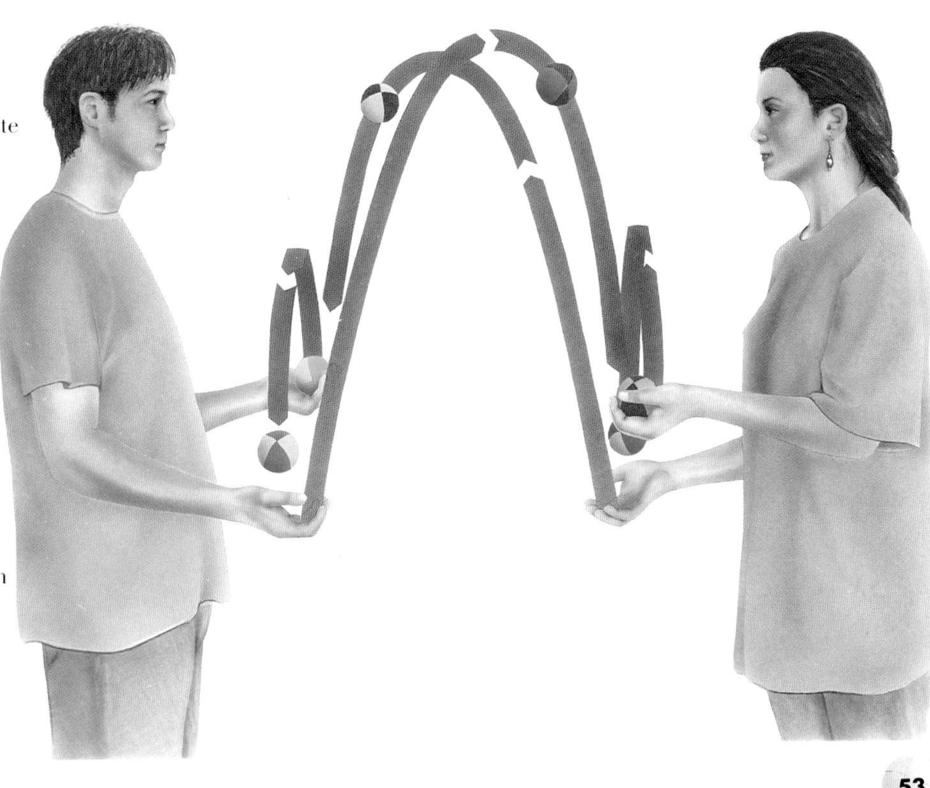

JUGGLING WITH RINGS

Juggling with rings is similar to juggling with balls or beanbags, but you must throw higher. You will, therefore, need more space above your head than is available in most rooms, and you have to find somewhere like a hall or gymnasium to practice. You can juggle outoors if it is a very calm day, but even a slight breeze will make the rings unstable.

Rings are as easy to use as balls or beanbags, and it is easier to juggle with five rings or more than with the same number of balls, because they can be held more comfortably and, being thinner, can be positioned more accurately without colliding in mid-air.

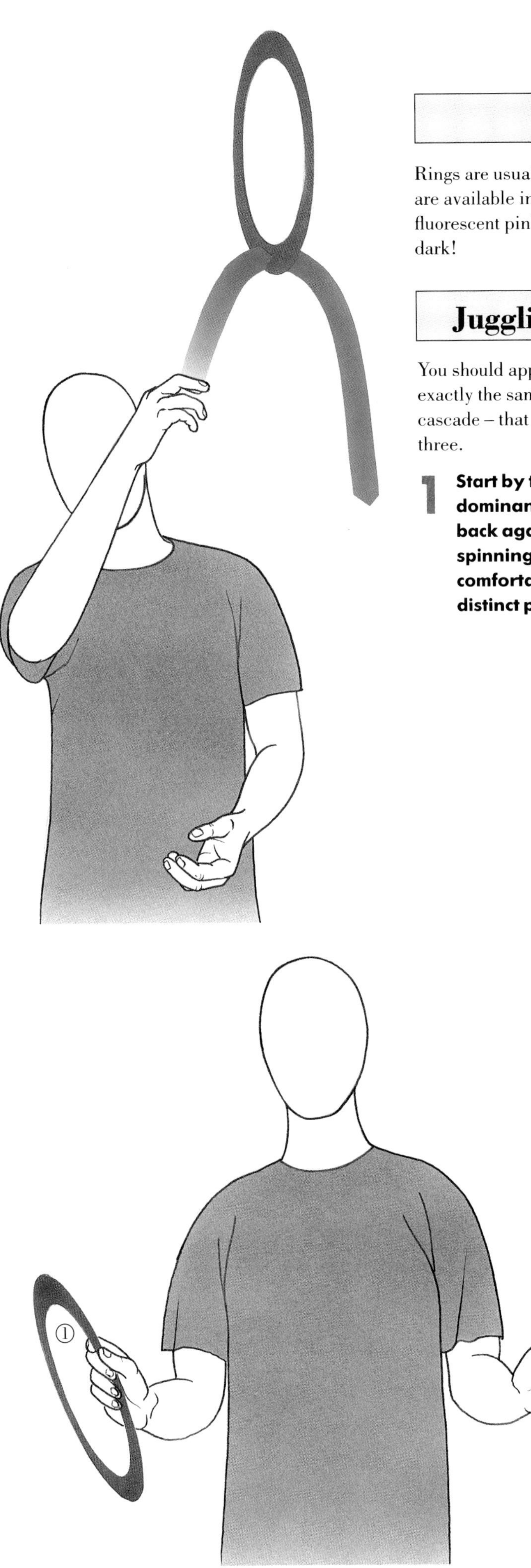

Equipment

Rings are usually made of plastic or plywood. Rings are available in a range of colors, including fluorescent pink and green, so you can juggle in the dark!

Juggling with Three Rings

You should approach juggling with three rings in exactly the same way as you learned the three-ball cascade – that is, begin with one ring and build up to three.

1 **Start by throwing one ring from your dominant to your subordinate hand and back again. Keep the ring stable by spinning it and throw as high as you comfortably can. There should be two distinct peaks.**

2 **Take a ring in each hand.**

3 **Throw the first ring from your dominant hand and, when it peaks, throw the second ring, just as you did with the balls or beanbags.**

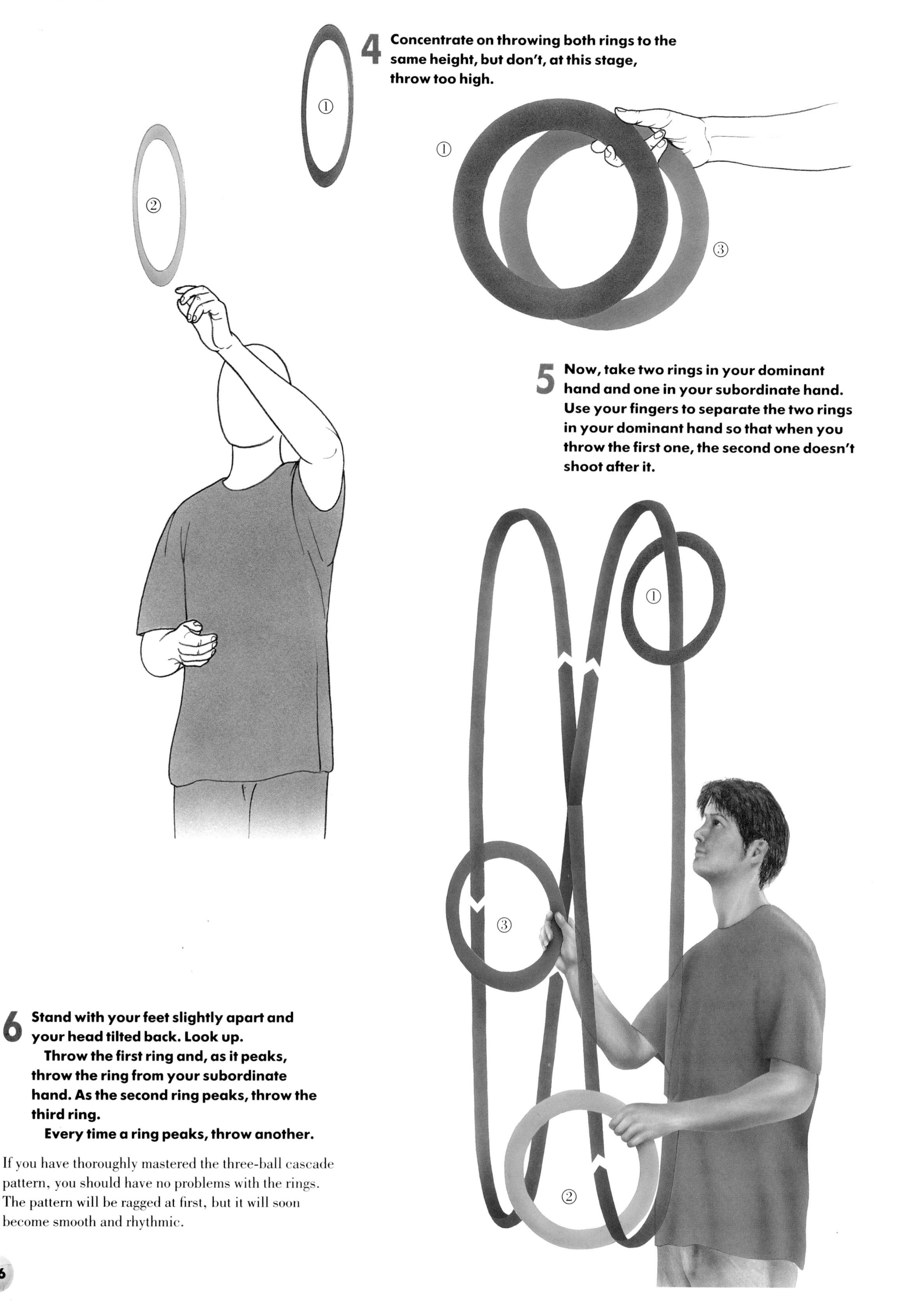

4 **Concentrate on throwing both rings to the same height, but don't, at this stage, throw too high.**

5 **Now, take two rings in your dominant hand and one in your subordinate hand. Use your fingers to separate the two rings in your dominant hand so that when you throw the first one, the second one doesn't shoot after it.**

6 **Stand with your feet slightly apart and your head tilted back. Look up.**

Throw the first ring and, as it peaks, throw the ring from your subordinate hand. As the second ring peaks, throw the third ring.

Every time a ring peaks, throw another.

If you have thoroughly mastered the three-ball cascade pattern, you should have no problems with the rings. The pattern will be ragged at first, but it will soon become smooth and rhythmic.

REMEMBER

- **Give each ring a spin as you throw it to help stabilize it and prevent it from wobbling.**
- **Reach up to throw and catch the rings.**
- **Tilt your head back and look up.**
- **Throw high – there should be two distinct peaks.**

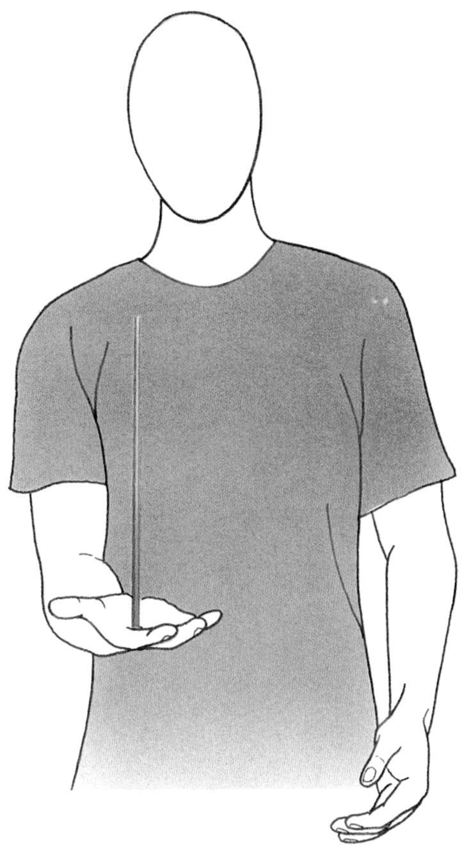

CATCHING A RING

When you feel more confident, try throwing the rings higher – you will be surprised how high they will go.

Bi-colored rings can look very effective in a stage performance. The basic rings that you buy are all one color, but you can buy special two-color rings or you can use spray paint or plastic adhesive tape to cover one side. As you juggle, change your grip between catches so that instead of gripping the rings in the normal way, your hands are turned in toward your body and your palms are facing up. Catch the rings on the palm and between your thumb and forefinger, but quickly bring your hand around to throw as usual, flicking the ring over so that the audience cannot see how you have done it.

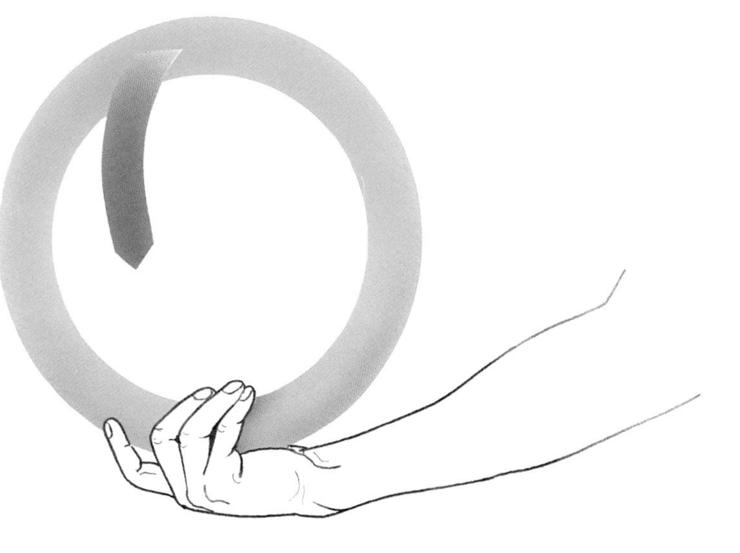

CATCHING AND FLIPPING THE RING OVER

Juggling with Four Rings

You juggle with four rings in exactly the same way as you juggled with four balls – that is, with two in each hand.

The most basic technique is to throw the rings simultaneously so that they are thrown from the mid-line of your body to the outside. However, you can easily adapt any of the four-ball patterns to four rings (see Chapter 4).

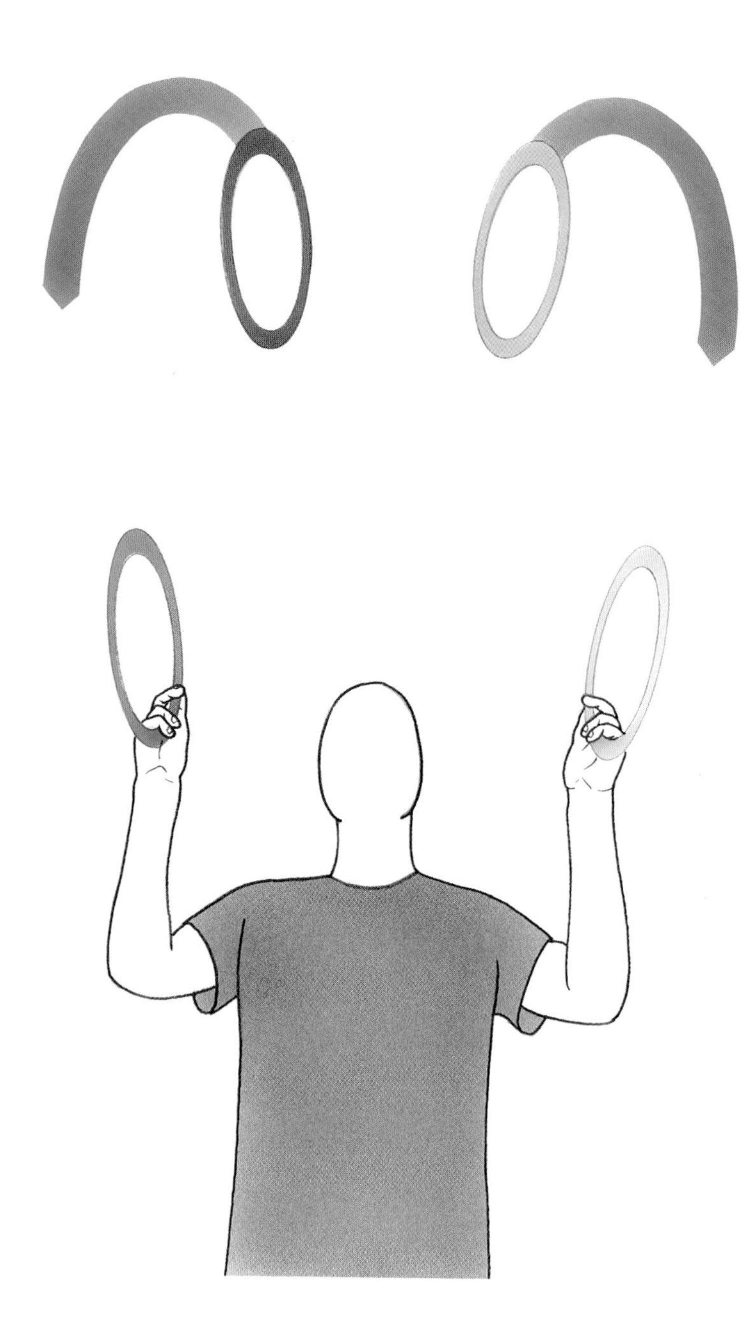

Juggling with Five Rings

As with five balls, you should begin simply by throwing three rings from your dominant hand. Throw the rings quickly and high to your subordinate hand, concentrating only on throwing and catching.

When you feel comfortable catching the three rings in your subordinate hand, begin to throw them back. Then you are ready to try with three in your dominant hand and two in your subordinate hand. You should throw the rings out at a slight angle, and you will need considerable space around and above you, because you have to throw them quite high to give yourself time to catch, pass, and throw.

1 **Holding three rings in your dominant hand.**

2 **As you finish your juggling routine, whether you are using three, four, or five rings, catch them in order, slipping them quickly over your head and around your neck.**

JUGGLING WITH CLUBS

When you feel that you have mastered the three-ball cascade pattern, you might want to consider moving on to juggling with clubs. Clubs will add an extra dimension to your juggling – three clubs are more difficult than three balls but easier than four balls. Some people find clubs easier to manage than balls, because the extra weight and the spin allow them to get a firmer grip.

Throwing a Club

Begin with one club and attempt to toss it in the air and catch it after just one spin.

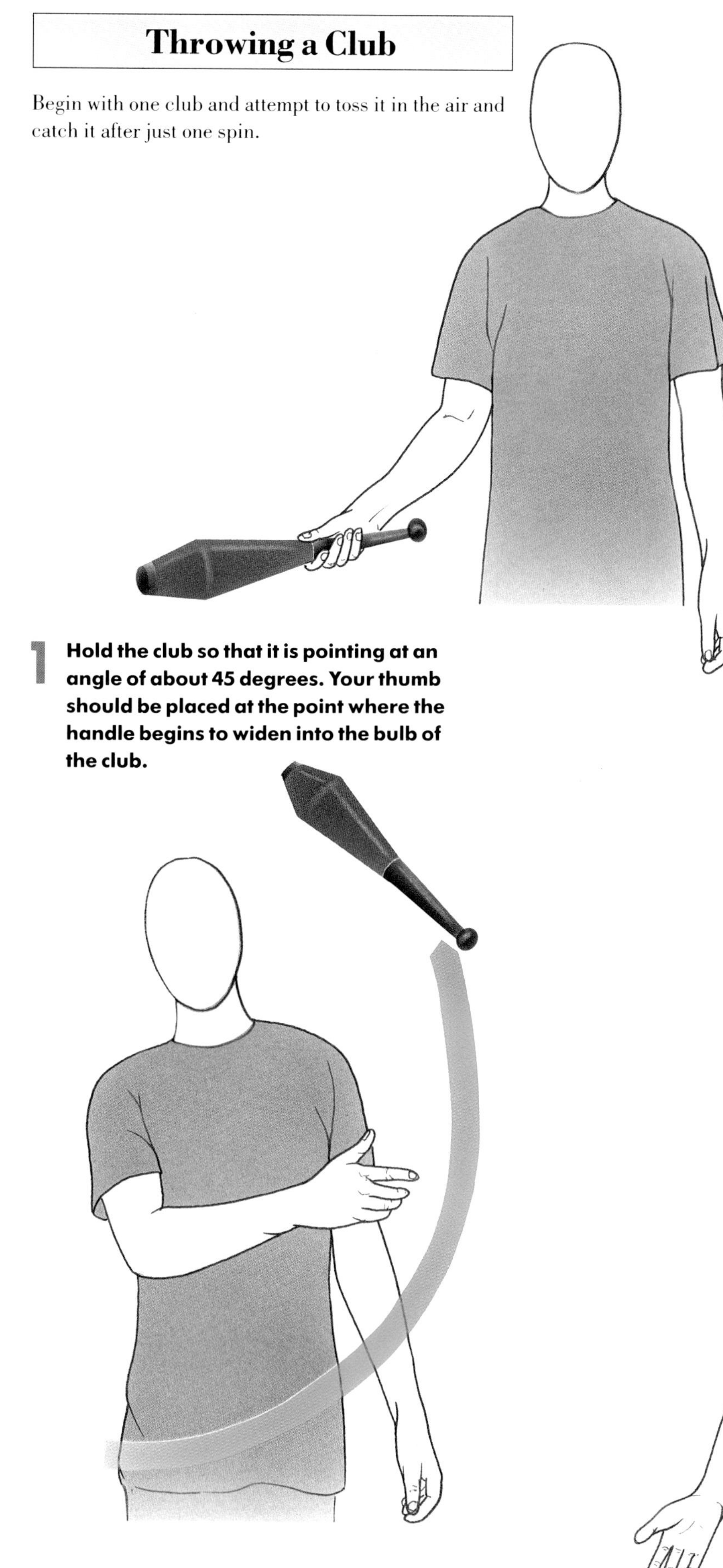

1 **Hold the club so that it is pointing at an angle of about 45 degrees. Your thumb should be placed at the point where the handle begins to widen into the bulb of the club.**

2 **Lower your hand slightly and then bring it up in a smooth scoop, letting go of the club when your arm is parallel to the ground. The movement should come from your arm, not from your wrist. Try to make the club rise vertically. You should not have to move your feet or duck your head as it returns to your hand.**

Equipment

Clubs are available in several weights, and some special lightweight ones are produced. You can also obtain clubs that are about three-quarters of the size of the standard kind, and these are suitable for children or for people who have small hands. Some clubs have terrycloth handles, which are comfortable to grip. They are available in a range of colors – red, green, blue, or white, for example – or you can even buy clubs that have stripes or other decorations on their bodies. If you are performing in public, you might want to use black or purple clubs with gold stripes!

One problem that arises with clubs that does not apply to juggling with balls is the amount of room you will need. When you begin to use clubs, you should throw them high to give yourself time to pass and catch. The ceilings in most houses are simply not high enough to give you sufficient space. In addition, clubs, even mini-clubs, that go astray can cause considerable damage. It is a good idea to begin outside – on the lawn is ideal – and always try to juggle on a soft, absorbent surface, such as carpet, matting, or grass. This will cut down the noise and the damage when you drop the clubs.

TAKE CARE

Always be careful with clubs – they can hurt. Don't get carried away trying double or triple spins until you are used to handling them.

3 **Catch the club between your thumb and fingers, and allow your arm to fall a little so that you do not jar your hand as you catch the club.**

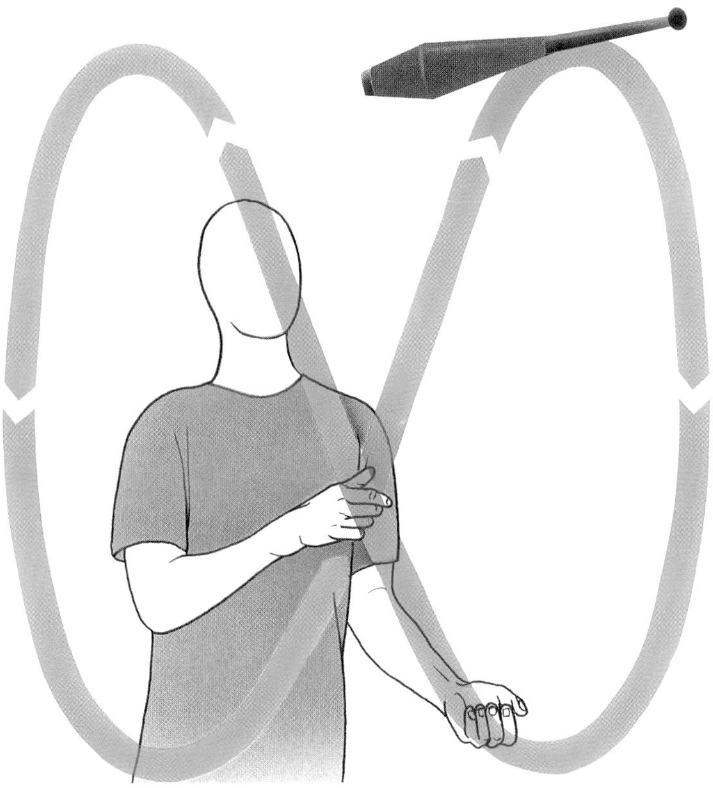

When you can toss a club and catch it after a single spin, try tossing the club from hand to hand, again making it spin just once.

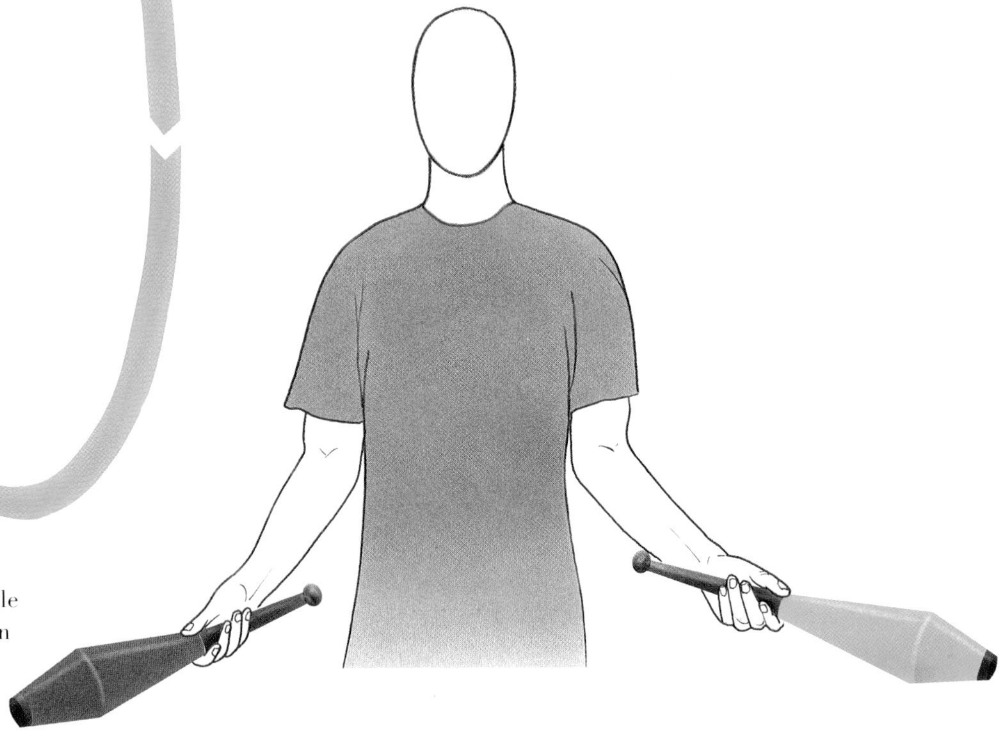

4 **You will have to throw the club across your body at an angle of about 45 degrees. You should catch it at an angle of 45 degrees away from your body and upwards from the ground. It is important that the height, speed, and spin of each throw is consistent.**

When you can throw and catch one club easily and smoothly, try juggling a cascade pattern with two balls and a club. This is a useful exercise, and, because you will already have mastered the three-ball cascade, you should find it relatively easy to incorporate a club into the pattern. In addition, if the club does go awry, you should be able to recover the pattern more easily than if you were already juggling with three clubs.

When you feel comfortable with one club, practice with two, one held in each hand.

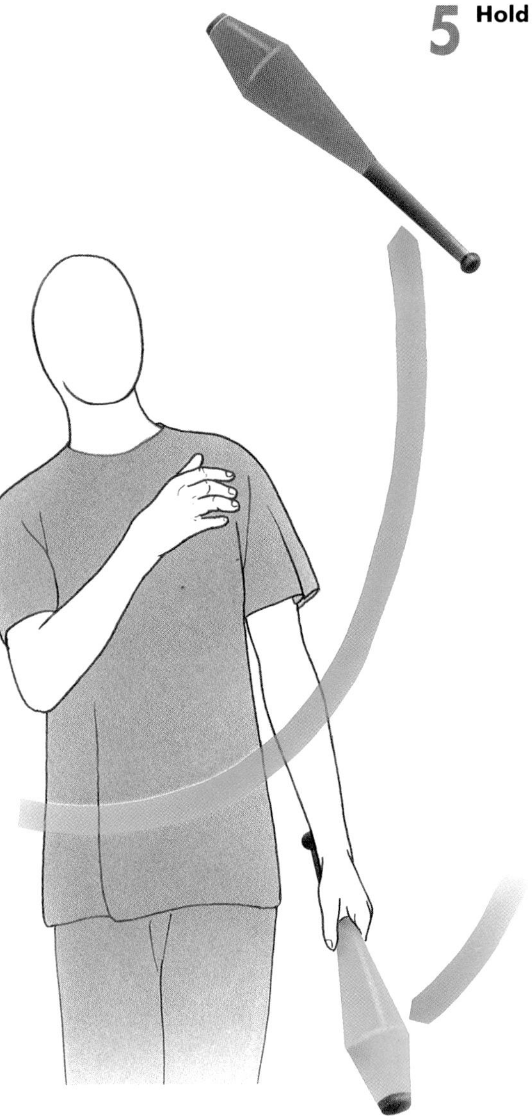

5 **Hold a club in each hand.**

6 **Throw the club from your dominant hand toward your subordinate hand. As the first club starts to turn, scoop and throw the second by bringing your subordinate hand down. Throw the club under the first one and toward your dominant hand.**

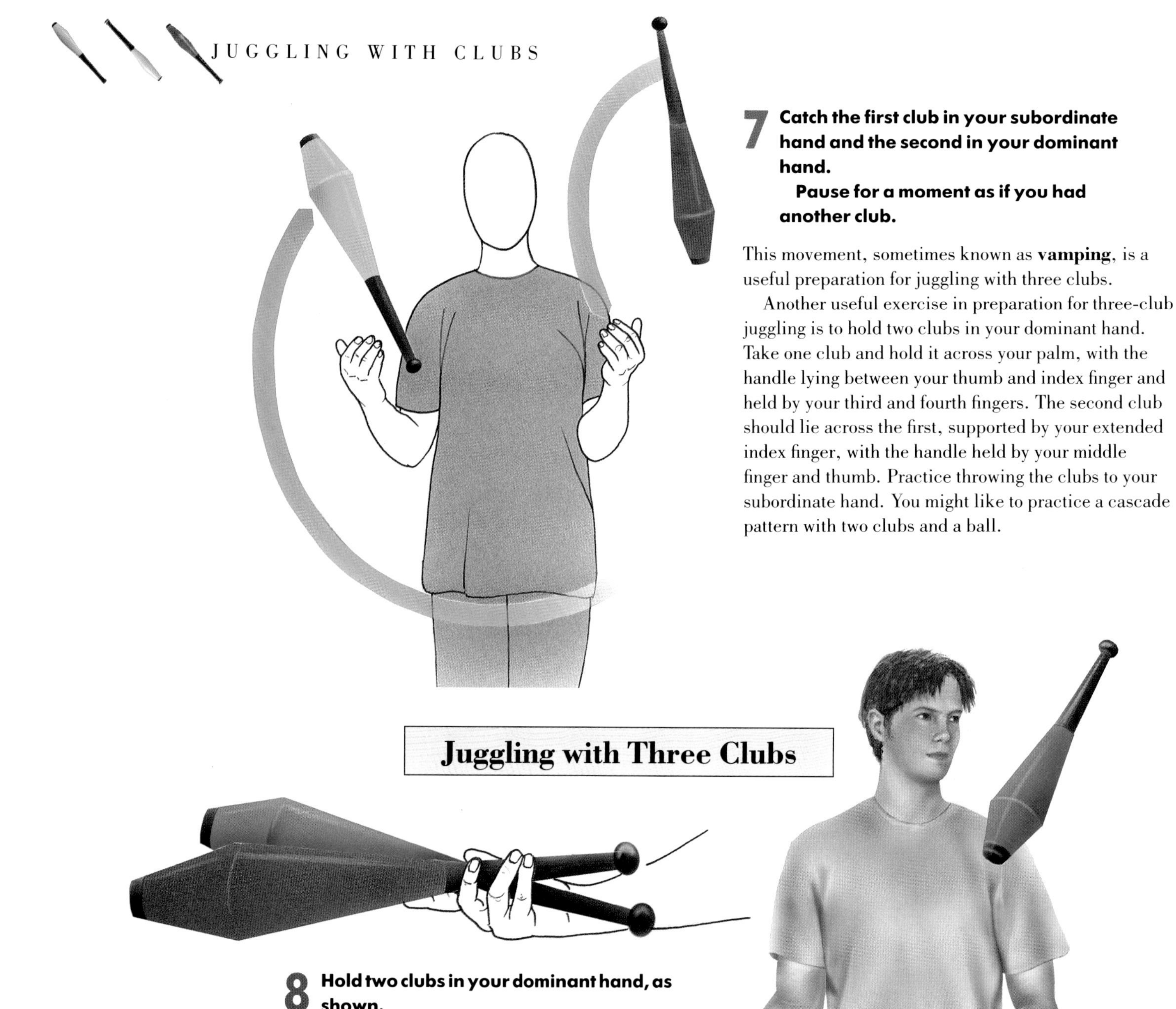

7 Catch the first club in your subordinate hand and the second in your dominant hand.

Pause for a moment as if you had another club.

This movement, sometimes known as **vamping**, is a useful preparation for juggling with three clubs.

Another useful exercise in preparation for three-club juggling is to hold two clubs in your dominant hand. Take one club and hold it across your palm, with the handle lying between your thumb and index finger and held by your third and fourth fingers. The second club should lie across the first, supported by your extended index finger, with the handle held by your middle finger and thumb. Practice throwing the clubs to your subordinate hand. You might like to practice a cascade pattern with two clubs and a ball.

Juggling with Three Clubs

8 Hold two clubs in your dominant hand, as shown.

At first, you should simply concentrate on catching the two clubs thrown from your dominant hand until you get used to the speed and rhythm. Now, try to throw and catch three clubs continuously. Relax your arms and shoulders and stand with your feet slightly apart. You will find it much harder if you are tense.

When you start to juggle with clubs, you have to throw them fairly high. As you practice, try to reduce the height of your throws and bring the pattern down. Your aim should be for the clubs to go no higher than the top of your head, and you should be able to bring your eyes down so that you can look straight ahead, through the pattern – this is important when you begin to pass clubs.

The pattern you want is similar to that of the three-ball cascade in that there are two distinct peaks and, in theory, the clubs should not collide. At first, however, your clubs are likely to crash into each other, and it will take you some time to get used to the height of your throws and the degree of spin. If your clubs continue colliding, you are either throwing too narrow a pattern, in which case you should extend the scooping motion, or your timing is wrong, in which case you should make sure that you are waiting until one club has peaked before you throw the next.

9 Throw the first club from your dominant hand. When the club turns, throw the club from your subordinate hand. When the second club turns, throw the next club from your dominant hand.

You may find that when you first start juggling with three clubs you just can't catch anything. You are probably giving them too much or too little spin. Go back to working with one club, first in your dominant hand, then in your subordinate hand, until the action is comfortable.

REMEMBER

- **Throw the clubs high when you begin to learn to give yourself extra time.**
- **Every time one club spins, throw the next.**
- **Alternate your hands – dominant, subordinate, dominant – and concentrate on smooth scoops.**

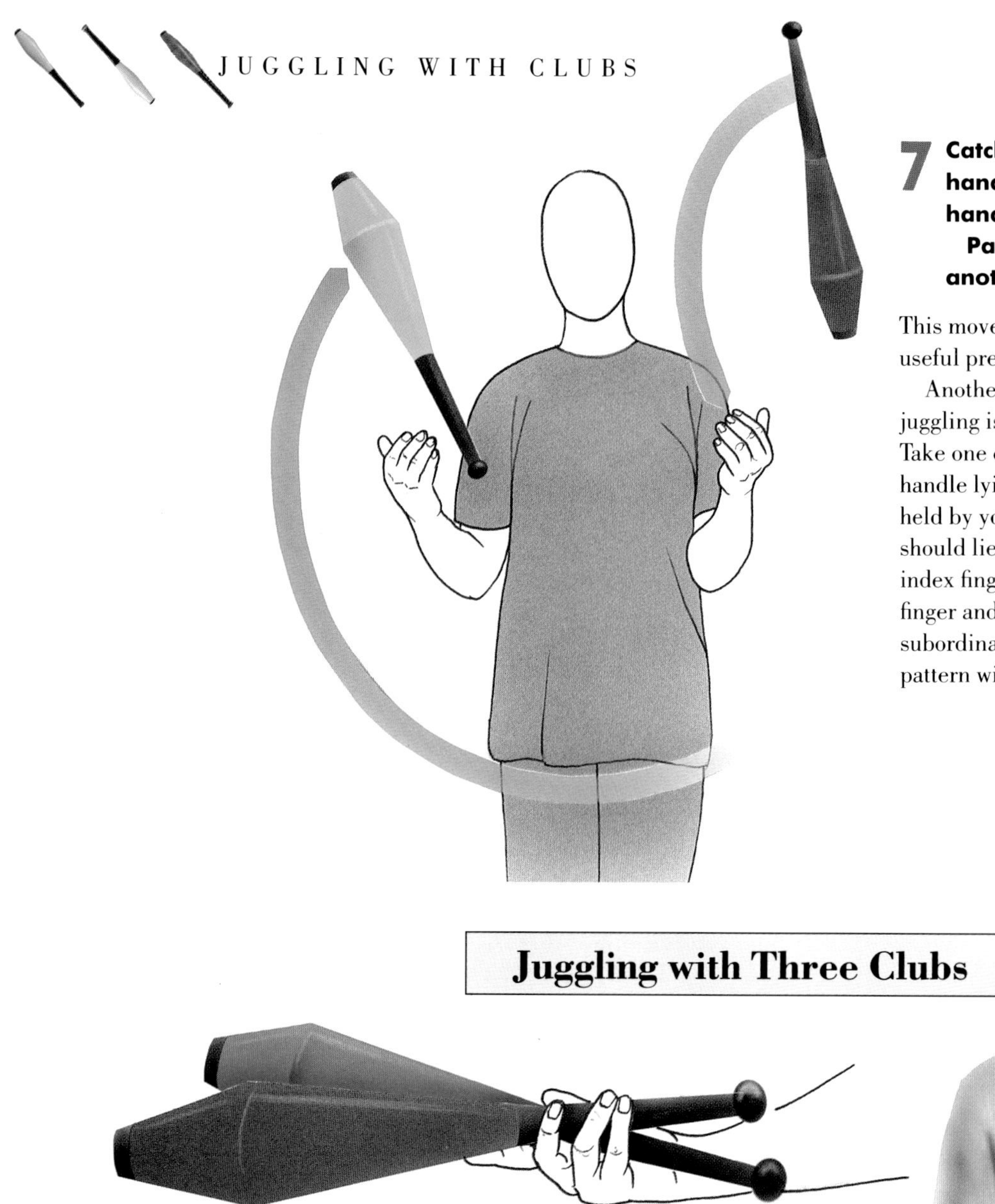

Three-club Variations

Many of the three-ball variations described in Chapter 2 – the reverse-cascade, columns, underarm throws, and so on – can be applied to clubs. Here, we will look at some variations that can be added to a basic three-club cascade.

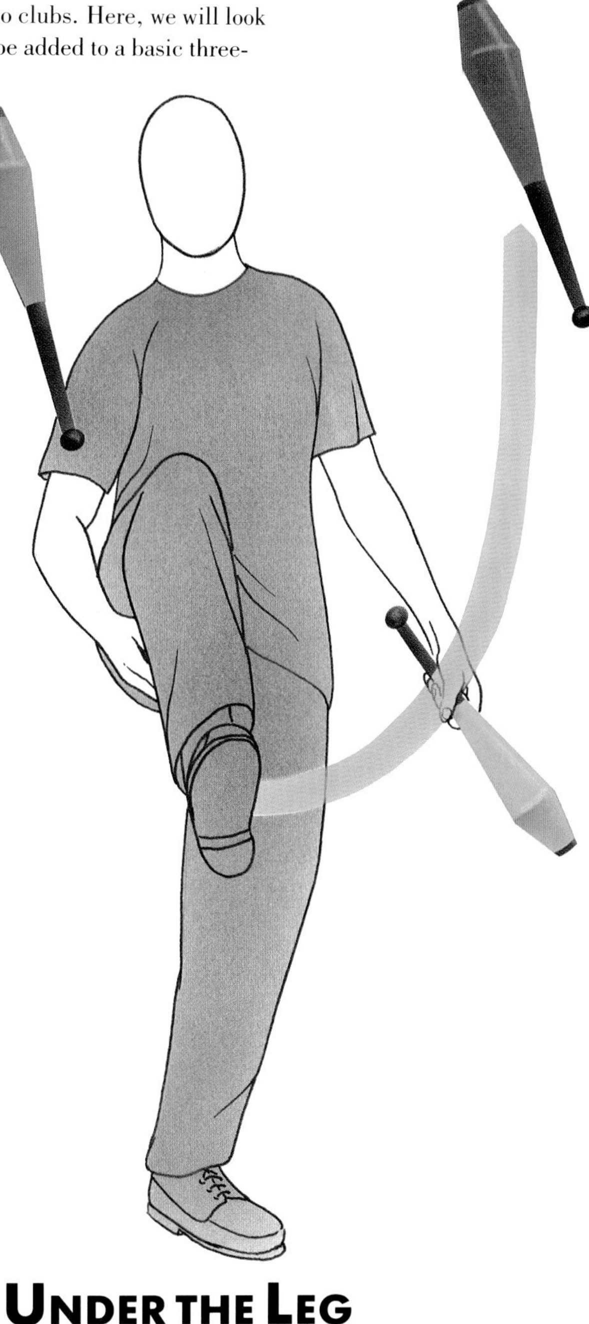

Double Spins

When you can juggle a three-club cascade, you might like to introduce variations into it by making the clubs spin twice. Bring your hand down a little lower than for a single spin and bring your arm up with more movement, both to impart the extra spin and to give additional height. You also need to twist your wrist. Practice with one club until you are always able to catch the club by its handle. When you feel confident that you can judge the speed and spin, introduce a second and then a third club into the routine, until you can juggle a full three-club, double-spin cascade.

Triple Spins

The triple spin depends on increased arm and wrist movements to give the extra height needed for the additional turn. Because the handles of juggling clubs stick out, you are more likely to catch the handle than the butt. Triple spins require considerable height – far more than you are likely to have in your rooms at home – and you may have a problem finding somewhere suitable to practice.

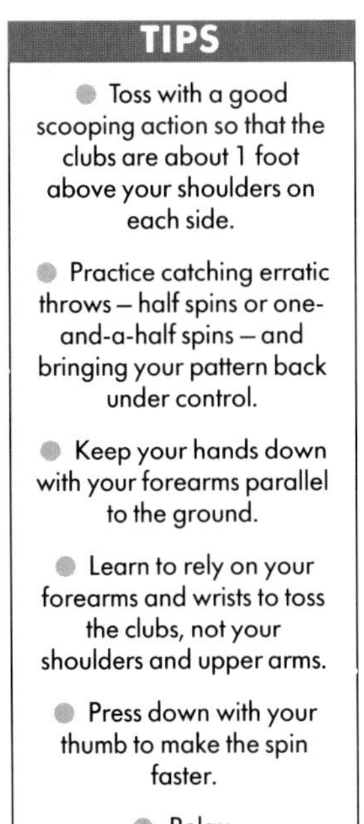

Under the Leg

This is a fairly simple movement, but begin by practicing with just one club. You will need to lower your hand more than usual. Raise the leg at the same side and toss the club upward, as if into the cascade pattern. When you come to do this in the middle of the cascade, you will find it helpful to throw the previous club slightly higher than normal to allow time to throw the next club under your leg. The aim is to toss a club under either leg during the basic cascade without interrupting the routine.

It is also possible to throw a club under the opposite leg – that is, if you were throwing the club with your right hand, you would toss it under your left leg. You will have to sway slightly to the right to do this successfully. Again, practice so that you can throw under each leg with equal ease.

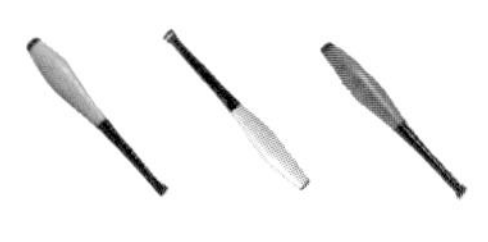

Behind the Back

Take one club and toss it from your dominant hand, behind your back so that you can catch it over the shoulder of your subordinate side and in your subordinate hand. You may find it helpful to lean slightly to your dominant side as you prepare to make the throw. So that the club's handle arrives neatly in your subordinate hand, you must slow the spin, by slowing down your wrist movement. Learn how to throw a club with your subordinate hand so that it comes over the opposite shoulder into your dominant hand.

When you introduce this movement into a three-club cascade pattern, it will help if you throw the previous club higher to give you some extra time for the maneuver.

This movement can look particularly effective if you make the club that you throw behind your back spin twice. You can also make the throw with every club that comes to your dominant hand, but it is probably more spectacular if you throw over each shoulder alternately so that your body is moving from one side to the other.

①

③

②

①

③

②

Placing a Club

Take advantage of the fact that when people watch jugglers they tend to keep their eyes firmly fixed on the objects in the air. They rarely look at the props in the jugglers' hands. At some stage during your routine, try throwing one of the clubs higher than usual and take the opportunity to tuck one of the other clubs under your arm, wedging it as close as possible to your body, or between your legs. Catch the falling club and stop juggling as if you had no idea where the missing club had gone.

Pirouette

A pirouette is a good opportunity to introduce a double spin into your routine. Remember that you will need extra space above you. Throw the club high with an extra wrist spin, and the additional time it takes to rise and fall will enable you to spin through 360 degrees before catching the club and continuing your cascade pattern. Focus on the club that is in the air, and keep the other two firmly in your hands while you spin around.

Club Balancing

When you are balancing an object, always concentrate on the top of the object. It helps, too, if you bend your knees slightly and if you have a perfectly clear area around you.

You can balance clubs on your chin, nose, forehead, or the top of your head. You may even have seen jugglers spin clubs on top of their heads. A slightly easier trick is to balance one club on top of another. Hold one club horizontally and balance a second club vertically on it so that the knob of the upright club is about halfway along the body of the horizontal one. Concentrate on watching the top of the vertical club.

When you can hold the two clubs steadily in this position, try including it in a juggling routine. Throw the clubs in a normal cascade pattern, but throw the club from your dominant hand with a double spin. Quickly place the next club to come to your dominant hand upright on the club in your subordinate hand and catch the double-spinning club in your dominant hand. You can resume the cascade pattern by throwing the club in your dominant hand up with a double spin, retrieving the balanced club, and continuing the cascade. Alternatively, you can end your routine with the balanced club.

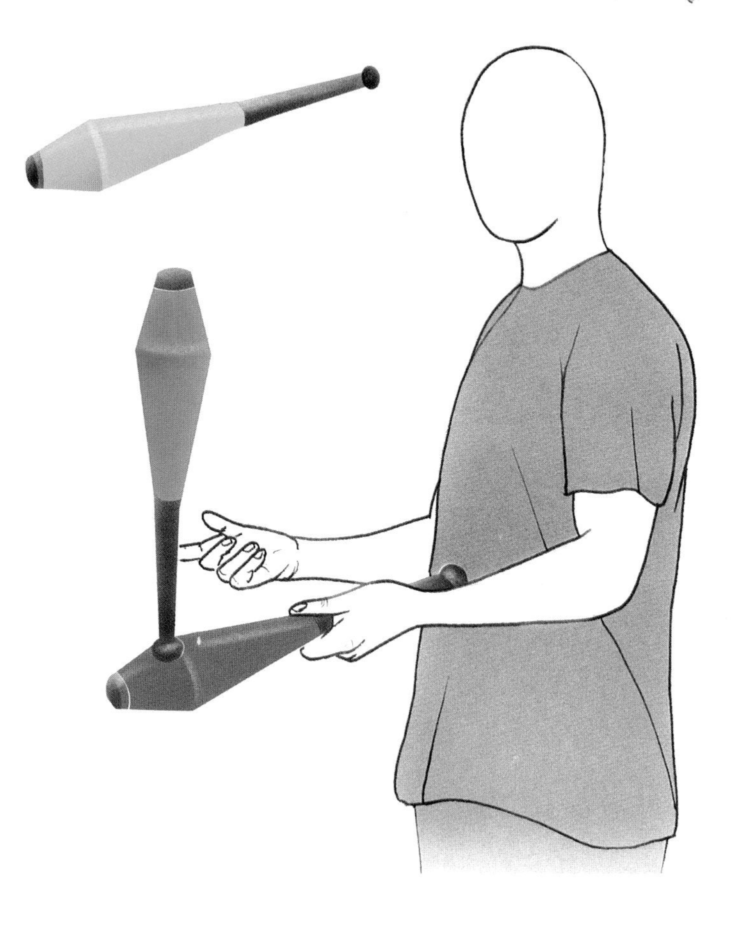

Kick-ups

You can use this trick either to start your routine or during a pattern. You will find it easier to do a kick-up if you are wearing sneakers or similar canvas shoes. Even bare feet are preferable to leather shoes.

Practice by placing the club on your foot. The handle should point inward, resting on your lower shin just above your ankle. Flex your toes upward to hold the club in place and step forward onto your other foot. Bend your knee slightly as you kick upward and back. The knob (at the end of the handle) should catch your shin, propelling the club upward, with a single flip, into your hand.

This is a useful way of escaping from an accidental drop during a routine. In fact, it can look so effective that you might want to consider incorporating it into a routine on purpose.

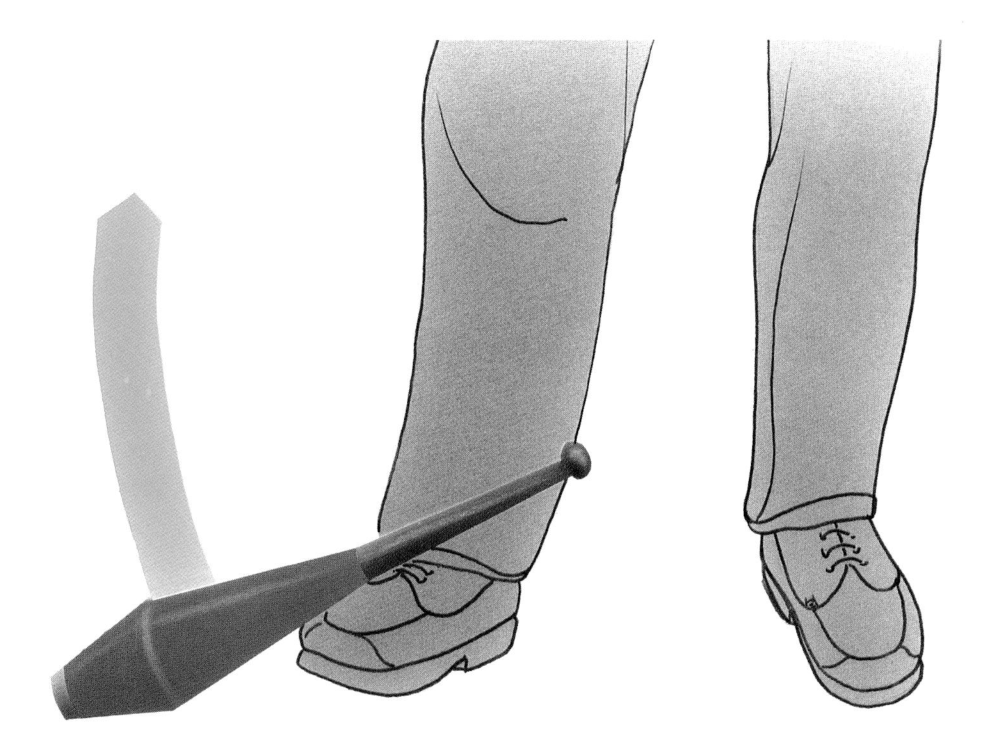

Fancy Starts

Two-club Start

Hold two clubs in your dominant hand and one in your subordinate hand. Toss a club from each hand into the air with a high single spin. The moment they are in the air, toss the third club straight up but to one side – in this instance, to the dominant side – of the other two, catch the first clubs in the hands that threw them, and move into a cascade pattern.

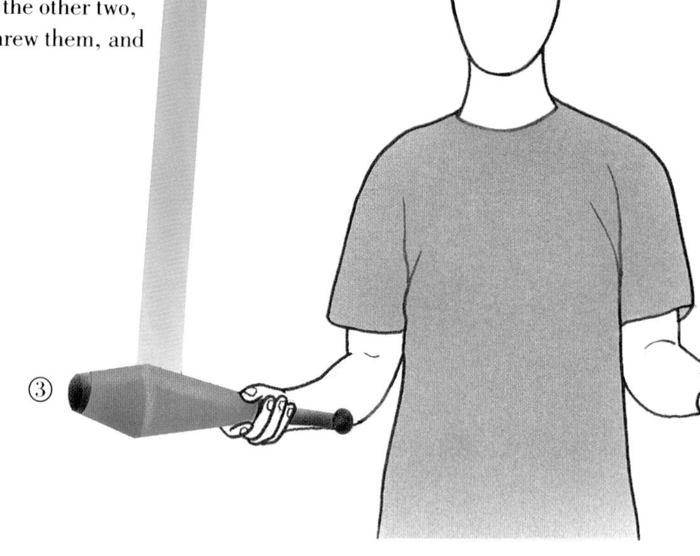

Three-club Start

Grasp the handles of the three clubs between your hands – two should be parallel with the third resting in the middle on top. The central club should extend over the ends of the other two by about 6 inches.

When you throw all three clubs up, this top club will travel farther and make one more spin than the other two. Therefore, you will have time to catch the other clubs and throw them before catching the third and beginning your cascade pattern. You must remember to throw the three clubs high.

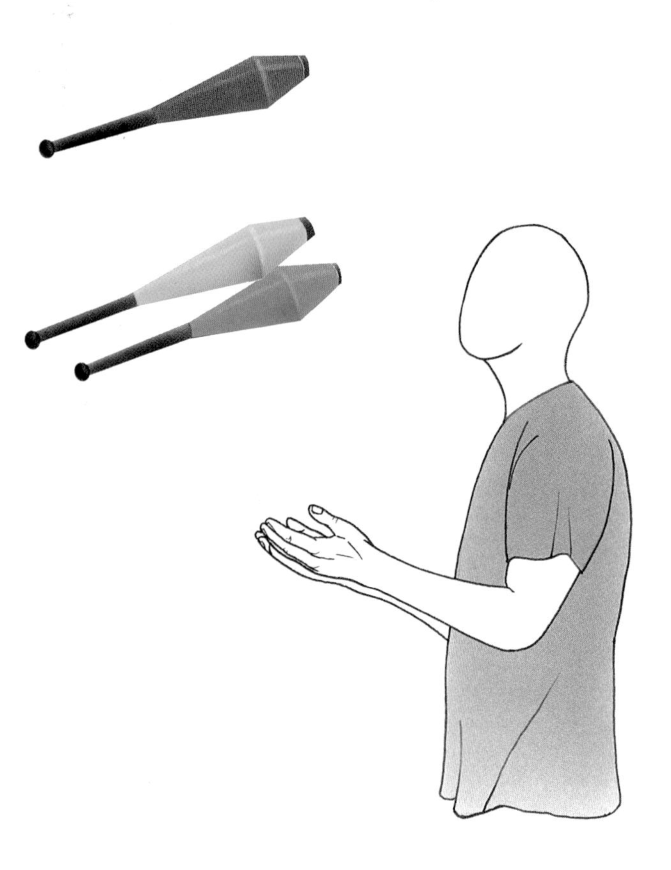

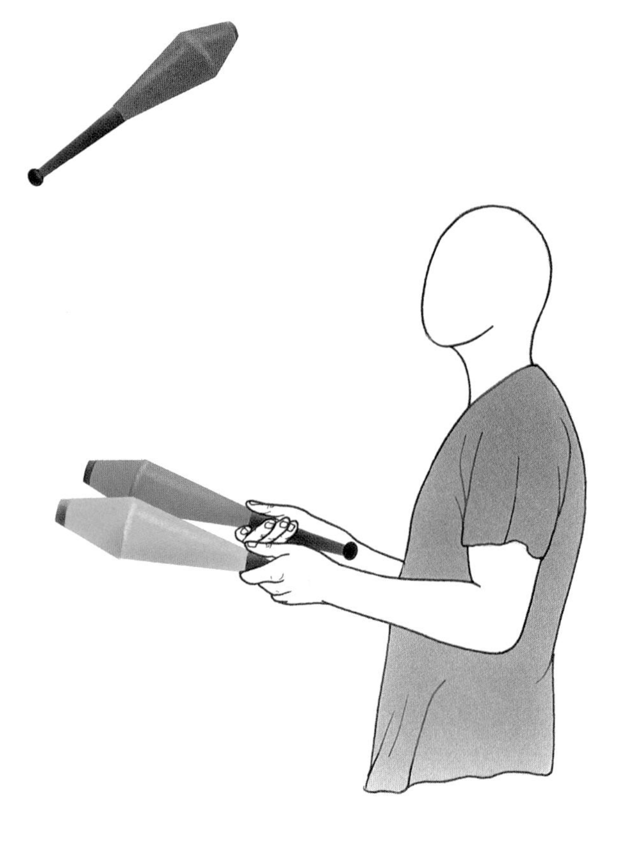

Club Endings

It is important to know how to stop a three-club cascade pattern without all the clubs falling on the floor. The simplest method is to catch the club that is in the air in your dominant hand on top of the club that is already there. Tuck the first club under the base of your thumb and stretch out your fingers. The two clubs will "smack" together as you catch them.

A triple spin of the last club will give you the extra time you need to pass the other two clubs to your subordinate hand so that you can catch the final club neatly in your dominant hand and finish your routine neatly. This kind of ending is more dramatic than simply catching two clubs in your dominant hand, and it is a suitably spectacular way to end a public performance.

Another possibility is to finish with a double or triple spin, which will also give you time to perform a pirouette before you catch the last club.

Alternatively, throw your final club with a double spin, transfer the club from your subordinate hand to your dominant hand (which is already holding a club), and make a V between these two clubs. As the third club falls, catch it in the V between the two clubs.

Juggling with Four Clubs

You can juggle four clubs in exactly the same way you juggle four balls – that is, with two clubs in each hand.

As you improve and become more competent with clubs, you may want to exchange your starter clubs for heavier and slightly faster ones. The ideal clubs are medium weight and spin, and these can be obtained with soft handles that help protect your hands.

When you start juggling with more than three clubs, it is essential that they are all the same size and weight.

1 Practice with each hand separately until you can throw the clubs with a single spin and catch them neatly. Keep your wrist movement to a minimum and try to maintain an even rhythm. Stop by catching both clubs in one hand.

2 When you can juggle with two clubs in each hand, try to use both hands at the same time. The difficulties will lie in throwing the clubs to the same height and in avoiding collisions. When you have mastered throwing the clubs at the same time, make the pattern more interesting by throwing the clubs at different times.

Another popular variation is called **splits**.

1 Throw two clubs up together to one side – say, to your right – and as they peak, throw the other two up together to your left. Move quickly back into position to catch the clubs on the right, throwing them straight back up, before moving again to catch and throw the ones on your left. Keep moving from side to side, catching and throwing as rapidly as you can.

As with four balls, you can throw clubs simultaneously from both hands, using outside or inside circles. Try this variation with double spins.

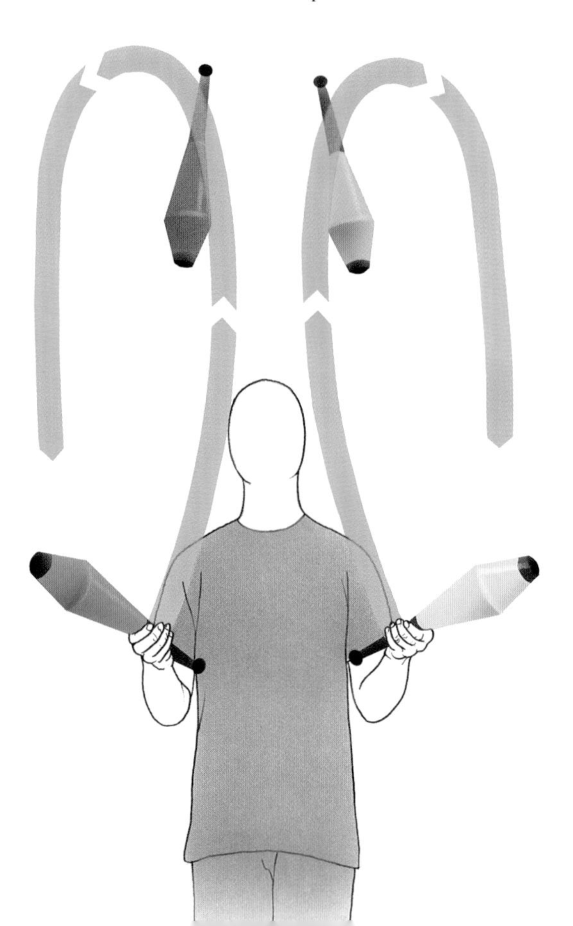

Juggling with Five Clubs

You will have to put in a lot of time and practice to master the technique of five-club juggling, but, as jugglers throughout the world have shown, it can be made to look easy once you know how.

GETTING STARTED

Begin with only three clubs.

1 **Hold three clubs in your dominant hand.**

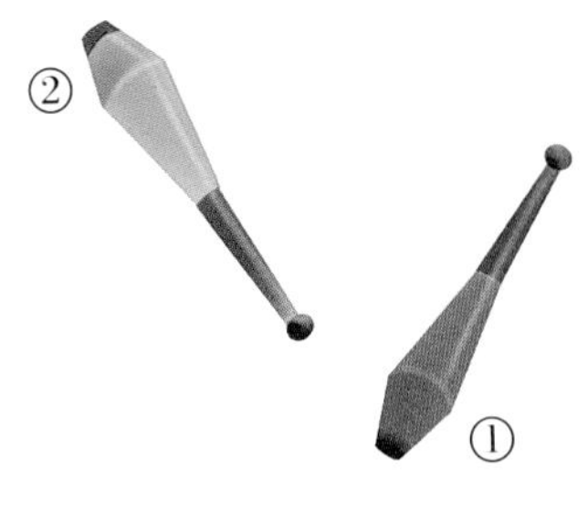

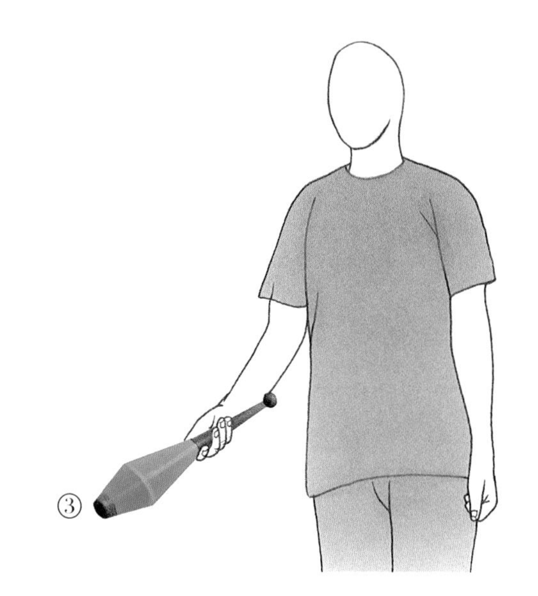

2 **Quickly throw the clubs high, one after the other, giving them double spins, and catch them in your subordinate hand.**

Pretend that you have five clubs and create a five-club pattern but with two empty spaces.

Without pausing, catch the clubs in your subordinate hand and throw them back to your dominant hand.

Concentrate on catching all three clubs in one hand when you finish.

3 **Now, take five clubs, three in your dominant hand and two in your subordinate hand, and go! This is when you will need all your juggling skills, accuracy, and speed. You must throw high and hard, bending your knees slightly to give extra momentum if necessary, and throwing each club from your dominant hand at the moment that a club comes into your subordinate hand.**

Don't stop to think. Successful five-club juggling depends on high, wide, and accurate throws and a good rhythm.

STOPPING

The normal method of stopping is to throw the last club extra high, usually with a triple spin.

Catch two clubs in each hand, but quickly tuck the two in your subordinate hand under your other arm so that you can catch the final club with your free, subordinate hand.

CLUB PASSING FOR TWO PEOPLE

Club passing between two people is basically the same in terms of timing and maneuvering as ball passing, and you should look at Chapter 5 for details. As with ball passing, it is essential that both you and your partner use the same dominant hand – that is, you must both lead with your right hand or with your left hand.

It is also vital that both you and your partner are proficient with clubs. Accuracy is all-important because of the extra size and weight of clubs, and you can increase accuracy by making sure that you throw in the correct way.

REMEMBER

- **The throw is made almost entirely by your arm action; there is only a minimum of wrist movement.**
- **If you use too much wrist action, the spin will be short and fast, and the club will be difficult to control and to catch.**
- **Throw with your palm upward and your fingers pointing towards the midline. Catch with your palm out and your fingers pointing to the outside.**
- **You may find it helpful to stand with the foot on your subordinate side slightly forward to help counteract the club's tendency to swing in toward your partner's body.**

1 Hold the club that is to be passed in your dominant hand, lowering your arm until the club is parallel to your leg.

Bring your arm up and forward, releasing the club when your arm is almost fully extended in front of you and at chest height.

The club should make one spin and be caught in your partner's subordinate hand, with the handle pointing downward. The catch should be taken in line with, but a little to the outside of, your partner's shoulder.

If both you and your partner concentrate on throwing accurately, catching should be relatively straightforward. A throw that is faster than normal or at an unusual angle will be difficult to catch and may make it difficult for your partner to recover in time to catch the next club.

Once the first club has been caught, bring your arm down in an outside sweep and throw the club in the usual cascade pattern.

Running Three

This routine is basically the same as the running three movement with balls described in Chapter 5. Begin with only one club.

TIP

Take your time. One of the attractions of this exercice is that you have to pause between throws. When you have caught all three clubs, juggle a cascade pattern with them for a while until you have gotten your breath back. Then, slowly throw them back to your partner. You can gradually increase the speed at which you throw and catch the clubs when you are ready.

REMEMBER

- **Drop your right arm to throw.**
- **Raise your left arm to catch.**

Running three offers opportunities to create and improvise additional variations. You could, for example, when passing the last club to your partner, throw it under your leg or between your legs. You could also throw it extra high with a double or triple spin – but don't forget that your partner has to catch the club and immediately take it into a cascade pattern.

1 **Throw the club from your dominant hand to your partner's subordinate hand (see above).**

Your partner should throw the club from his/her subordinate hand to his/her dominant hand with a single flip, and throw it back to your subordinate hand.

Catch the club in your subordinate hand and, with a single flip, throw it to your dominant hand.

2 **When both you and your partner feel comfortable passing one club to and fro, move on to three clubs. When the third club is thrown to your partner, he/she can begin to juggle a cascade pattern or return the clubs immediately to you. As with balls, you can build up a continuous passing routine in which you throw all subordinate-hand catches across your chest to your dominant hand while all dominant-hand catches are thrown to your partner's subordinate hand.**

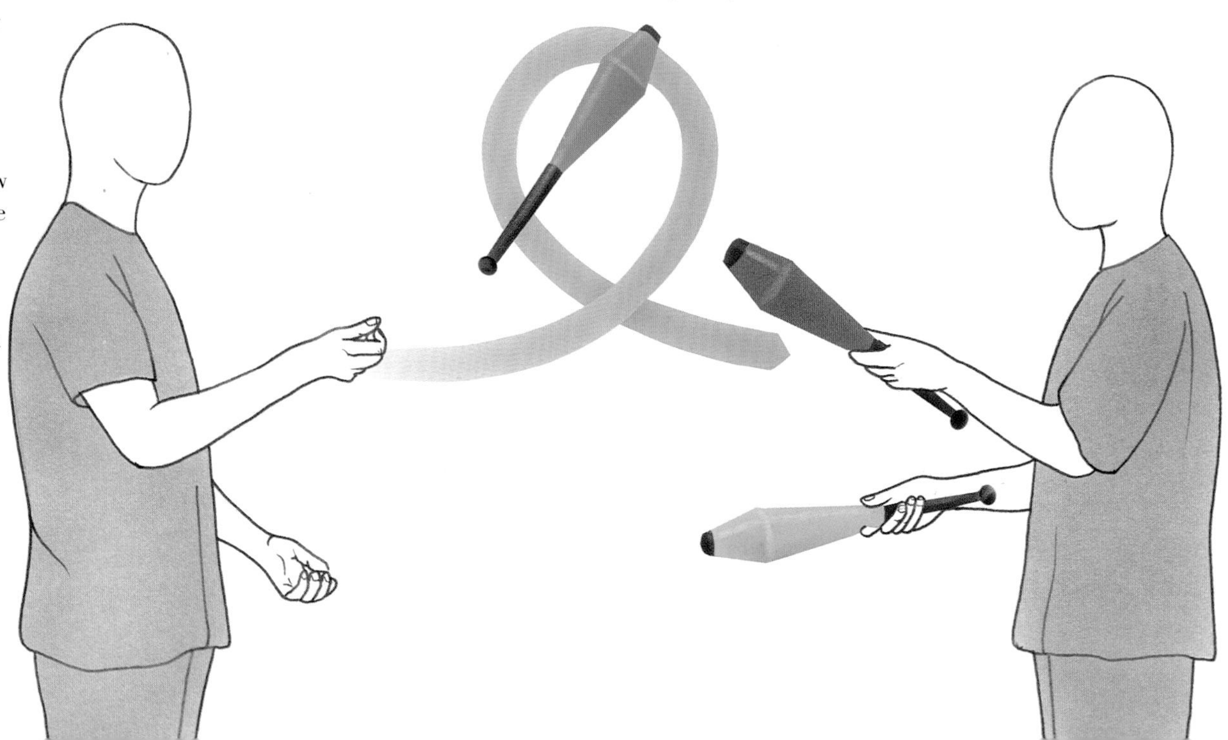

Three-club Variations

Over the Head

Your partner should stand behind you.

1 **Throw all three clubs over your head in rapid succession so that your partner can catch them and continue juggling with them.**

Be careful when you do this! This routine can safely and easily be done with balls.

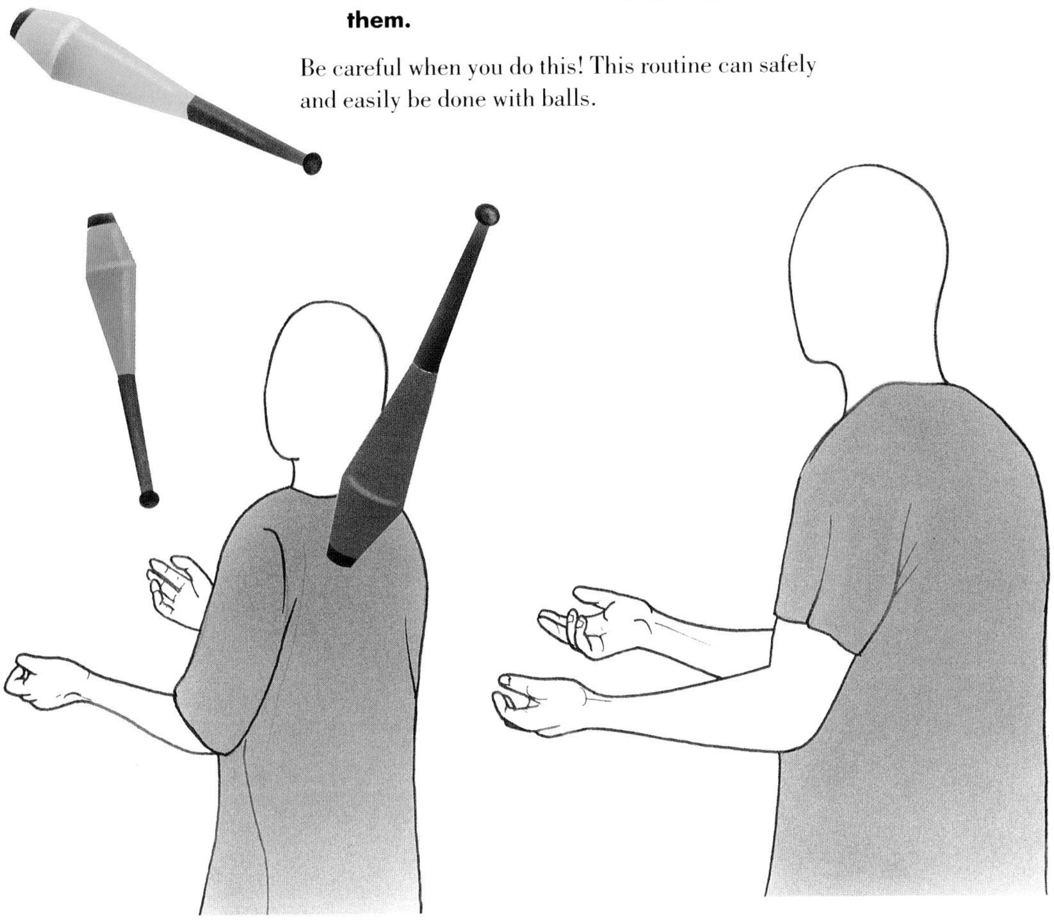

TIPS

- The way you stand is important. Keep your weight evenly distributed over both feet, but with the foot on your subordinate side slightly forward.
- Just before you throw, bring your dominant arm down so that the club is parallel to your leg.
- Use your full arm when you throw, using the pressure of your thumb to push down on the handle of the club just below the knob.
- Try to make the same throw each time – consistency of speed and angle is vital.
- Throw straight so that the knob and butt of the club turn in a single plane and are not tilted outward or inward.
- Keep your body movements to a minimum.

Side by Side

This is another routine that can also be performed with balls.

1 **Stand close to your partner. Each of you should put your inside arm behind your back. If you are standing on the right, you will use your right hand only, while your partner will use only his/her left hand. You should be able to juggle a cascade pattern, each of you using just one hand.**

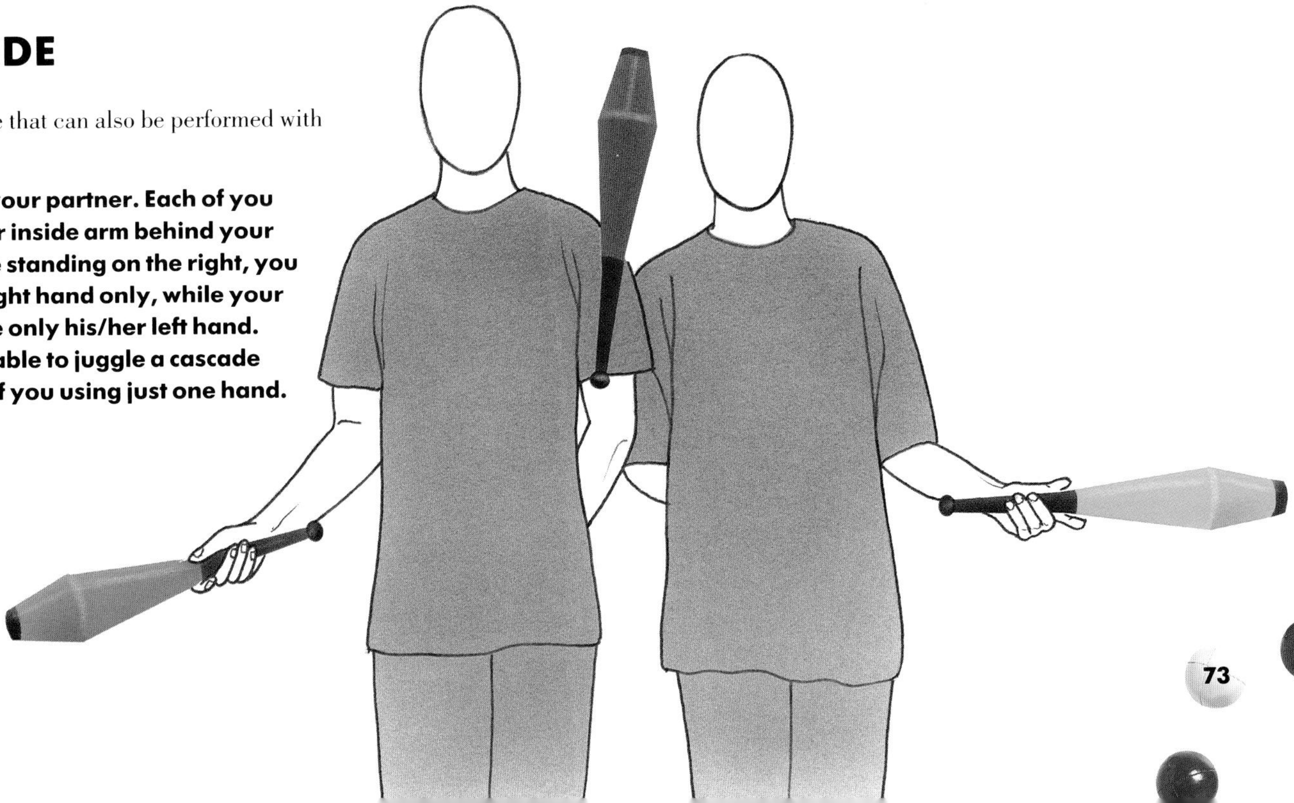

Passing Six Clubs

When you and your partner feel comfortable with running three, you should move on to passing six clubs. You will already have gotten the feel of this when you were working with six balls, but six spinning clubs look very impressive, and this is a spectacular routine to include in public performances.

1 **Both you and your partner should hold two clubs in your dominant hand and one each in your subordinate hand. Stand facing each other with the clubs raised.**

Begin to juggle a cascade pattern at the same time (see Chapter 5 for advice on starting together).

Count out loud, "One-and-two-and-throw, one-and-two-and-throw," so that you each toss every third club from your dominant hand to your partner's subordinate hand.

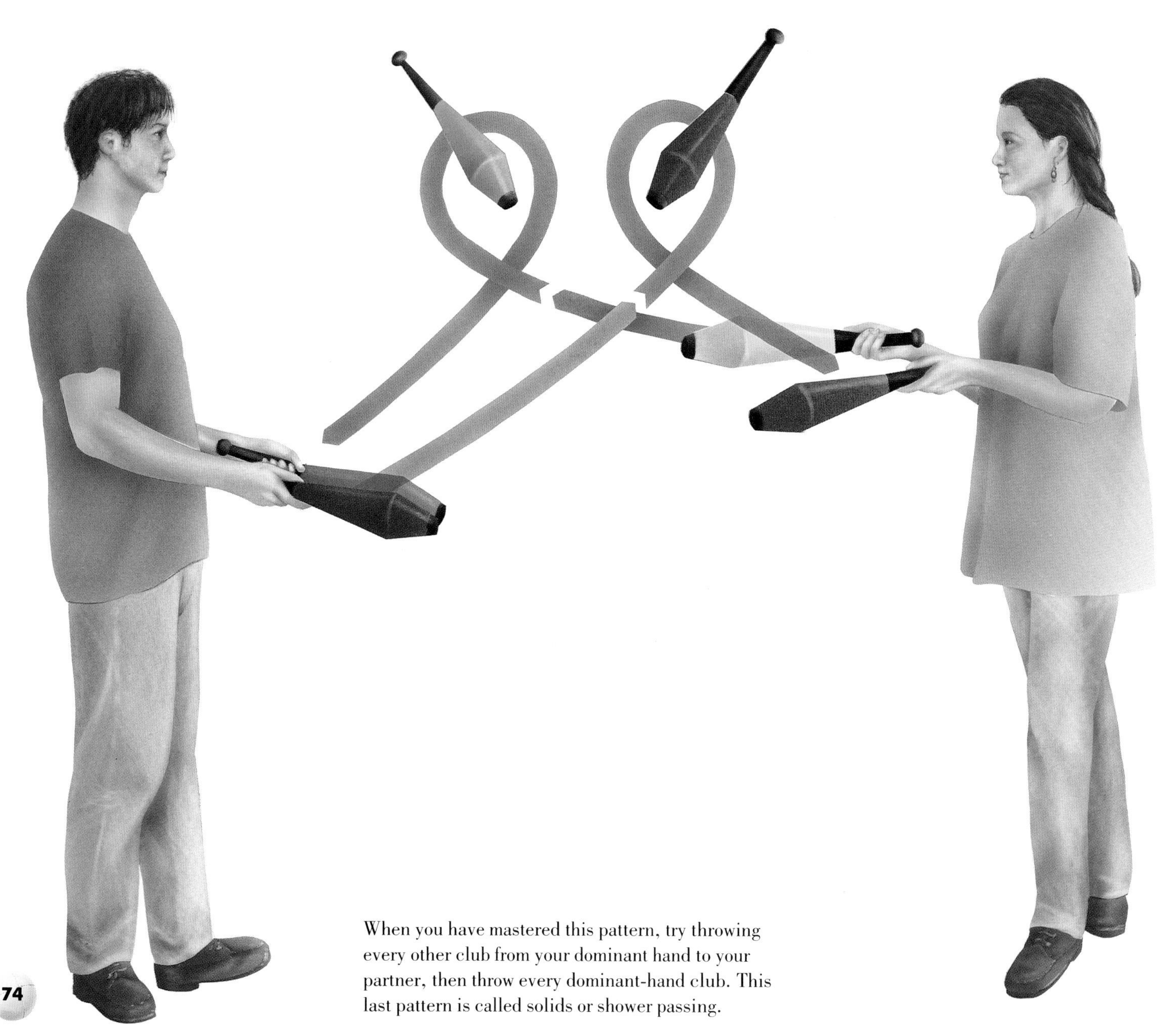

When you have mastered this pattern, try throwing every other club from your dominant hand to your partner, then throw every dominant-hand club. This last pattern is called solids or shower passing.

JUGGLING WITH OTHER OBJECTS

This chapter is an introduction to three popular juggling-related skills that are recognized as part of the juggler's craft – devil sticks, diabolo and plate spinning. Juggling is all about manipulating objects, and although the three skills described in this chapter are not always regarded as juggling, they share many of the same characteristics. The equipment you will need can probably be bought from the same supplier as your beanbags, clubs, rings, and juggling balls. You will also find that all three of these skills will combine well with your other juggling routines and contribute to a varied and interesting act. Although there are several other related skills, these three are the most popular and also the easiest to learn to control.

Devil Sticks

The equipment comprises three sticks. Two of these are about 19 inches long and about ½ inch in diameter; they are generally encased in rubber or have a terrycloth grip. The third stick is 25–30 inches long and has a central diameter of 1–1½ inches, broadening toward each end to a diameter of 1½–2 inches. It is usually covered in thin material or plastic and may be decorated.

Begin by standing the large stick on end in front of you and by holding the other sticks, one in each hand. Do not grip them too tightly.

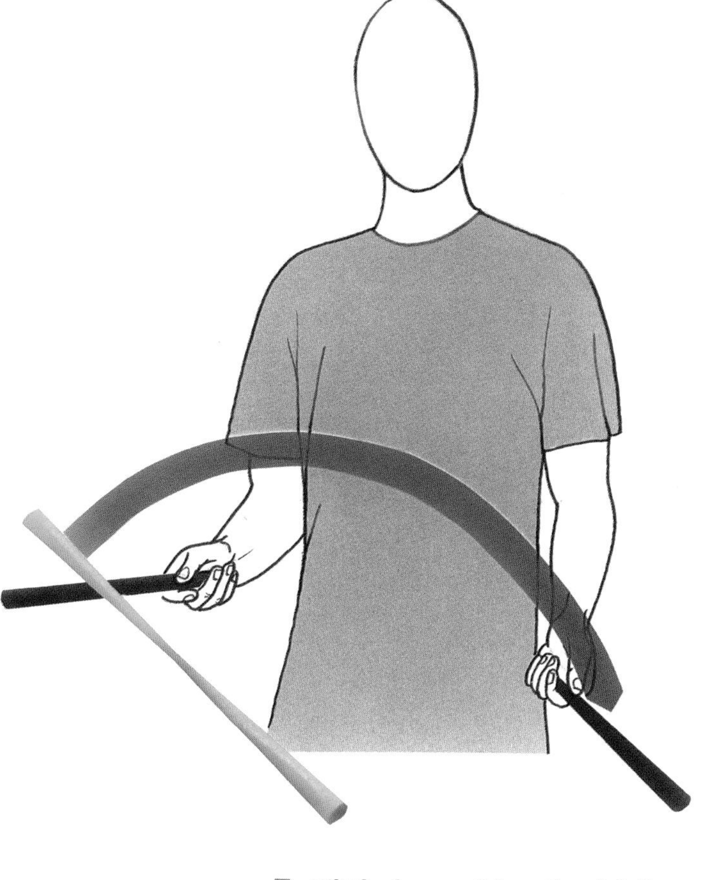

TIPS

- If the large stick rolls over the top of your hand-stick, you are striking it too close to the central "waist." Aim a little higher.
- If you think you are losing control of the large stick and that it is moving too quickly, you are probably striking it too close to the top. Aim a little lower.
- If the large stick seems to be running away from you, your hand-sticks are probably not parallel and horizontal. Try to avoid making them into a V-shape.

1 Tilt the large stick so that it falls.
When it reaches an angle of 45 degrees, knock it back with one of the hand-sticks, hitting it above the central "waist."
As it falls to the other side, knock it back with the other hand-stick.

Diabolo

You have probably seen children playing with small diabolos – they look like two cones stuck together at the narrow ends and balanced on a string held between two sticks. The toy, which works on a similar principle to the yo-yo, is thought to have originated in China, and it was popular with children at the end of the 19th century.

Most diabolos are made of rubber or plastic, and you will find that the heavier and larger ones are the most versatile. There is a humming diabolo, made of bamboo, which makes a humming noise as it is spun – the faster it moves, the louder the noise it makes.

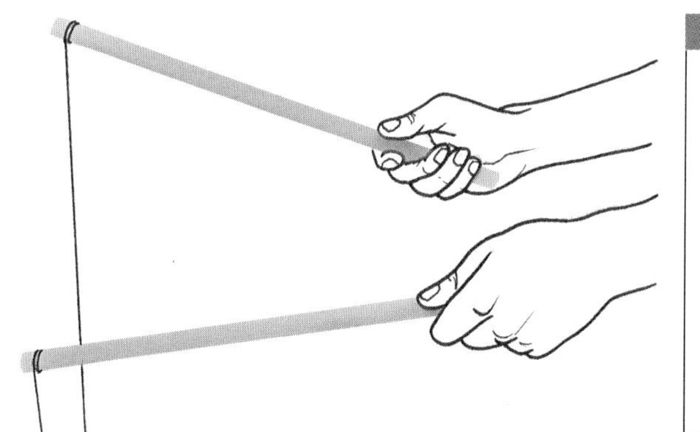

TIP

If the diabolo tilts and looks as if it is going to fall off, move your left hand in the direction in which the diabolo is tilting – that is, if the diabolo tilts away from you, move your left hand forward in a horizontal plane; if the diabolo tilts toward you, draw your left hand back toward your body.

1 Lay the diabolo on the ground in front of you with the string or cord below the "waist."
Take a stick in each hand and lower your right hand until it is close to the diabolo.
Take up the slack in the cord by raising your left hand.
Sharply raise your right hand upward. This movement of your right hand imparts an anti-clockwise spin to the diabolo as it moves along the cord to your left hand.
Drop your right hand so that the diabolo falls back; quickly raise your right hand again to spin it back.

REMEMBER

- **Your left hand hardly moves at all.**
- **Your right hand controls the spin of the diabolo through smooth but quick movements.**

REMEMBER

- **Hold your hand-sticks horizontal and keep them parallel to each other.**
- **Aim to strike the large stick at a point mid-way between the central "waist" and the top.**
- **Use your hand-sticks to throw and toss – don't hit.**

Your aim is gradually to raise the large stick from the floor by knocking it upward as well as sideways. The shape of the large stick makes this possible.

You can speed up the process by hitting the large stick below its central "waist" with one of the hand-sticks at the same time that you hit it above the center with the other hand-stick. If the large stick begins to roll horizontally, push one of the hand-sticks forward until the large stick has straightened itself.

You can encourage a horizontal roll and use just one hand-stick to control the large stick, striking it on the underside as it spins around. You can also keep the large stick spinning vertically by tapping it gently slightly below the central point each time it moves towards the horizontal.

If you find that the diabolo begins to swing around, move so that your body is always facing its end.

In order to toss a diabolo, you must make sure that it is spinning so fast that it will continue to spin while it is in the air and when it is caught again on the string. If it is not moving fast enough, it will tumble end over end, and you will not be able to catch it. When the diabolo is spinning quickly, bring your hands together, then separate them quickly so that the string is taut. This will flick the diabolo into the air. Aim for a smooth but quick action – the quicker and larger it is, the higher the diabolo will rise.

Catch the diabolo at the right-hand end of the string, holding your stick high so that you can aim the string at the central portion of the diabolo. Hold the sticks apart but, as the diabolo lands, bring your hands together to slacken the tension on the string so that the diabolo sags into the string rather than bouncing off it. Begin to build up the spinning motion immediately.

You can try bouncing it off the string without spinning it between catches. Catch it at the right-hand end of the string, keep the string taut, and allow the diabolo to run along the string toward your left hand before flicking it off again. If you have a partner, you can try passing the diabolo to and fro.

When the diabolo is spinning fast, you can make it climb the string in defiance of gravity. Gradually raise the left-hand stick to head height. The diabolo will be near the right-hand stick, which should be used to loop the string around the center. As you move your hands apart and tauten the string, the diabolo will rise.

Plate Spinning

Special plates and sticks can be bought from juggling supply shops and also from some toy shops.

The trick is to catch the point of the stick in the ridge on the underside of the plate.

1. **Hold the stick upright and point your forefinger up along it.**

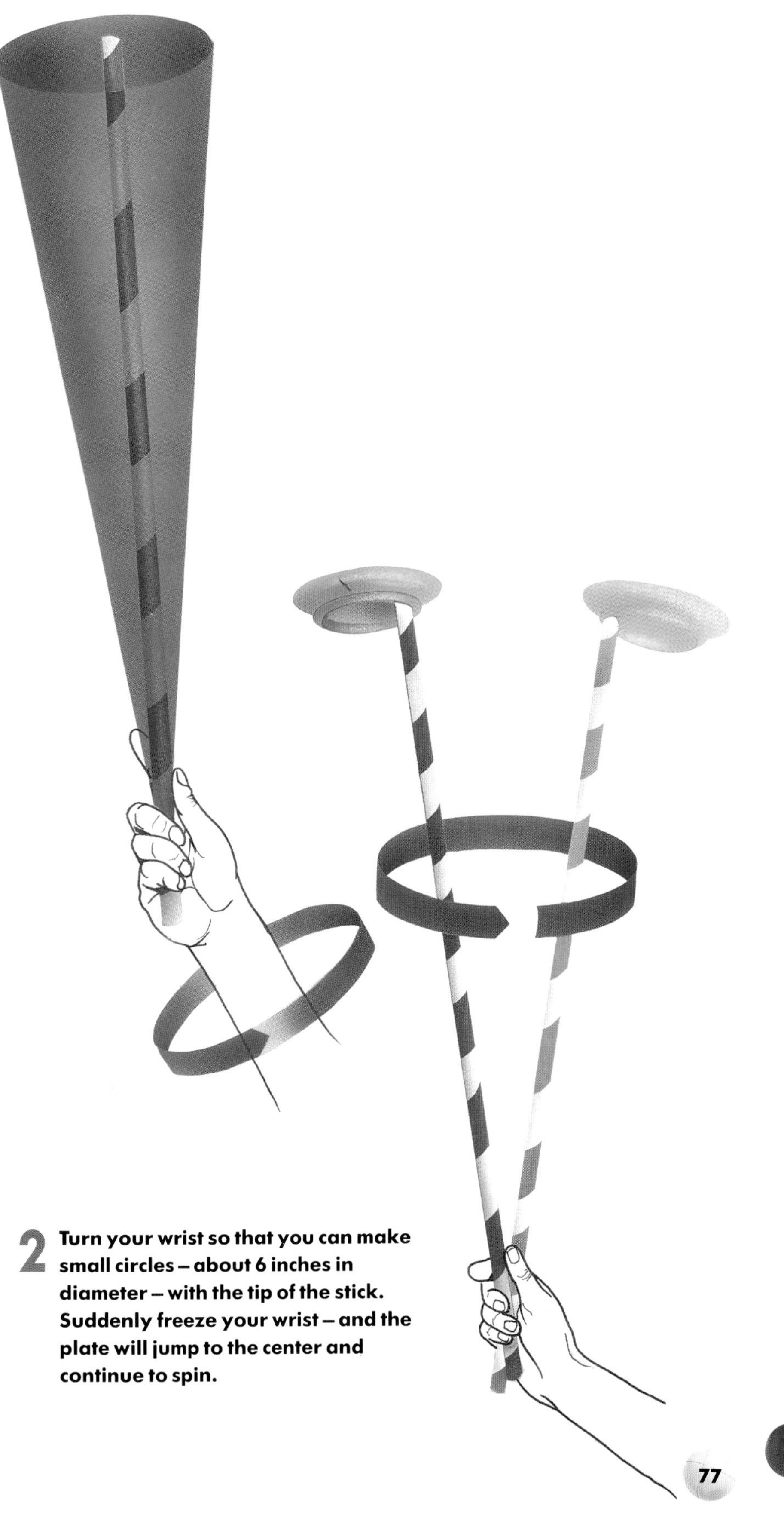

2. **Turn your wrist so that you can make small circles – about 6 inches in diameter – with the tip of the stick. Suddenly freeze your wrist – and the plate will jump to the center and continue to spin.**

Putting an Act Together

Most people take up juggling, not because they want to become professional jugglers, but because they enjoy the challenge involved in acquiring new skills and because they gain great satisfaction from developing the dexterity they have gained. However, there is no denying that juggling can be spectacular. A time may come, therefore, when you feel sufficiently confident of your prowess to put on a performance for your friends or for a children's party.

The main difference between practicing juggling and putting on a performance is that when you are practicing, you are trying out new movements or patterns or pushing yourself to achieve a record number of throws and catches. When you perform in public, your aim is to entertain. This means that your act will be made up of routines and patterns that you have practiced until you are as nearly perfect as possible. It also means that you will want to introduce as much variety as you can into your act to keep your audience's attention.

Even if you have no urge to perform in public, it is sometimes useful to know how to complete a smooth transition from one pattern to the next. Instead of practicing individual movements, you can weave them together, working on patterns that flow together. Working out smooth transitions from one trick to the next is another way in which you can make practicing interesting for yourself.

If you are going to appear in public, it is a good idea to practice in front of a mirror or a friend. Best of all, if you have access to a video camera, record your act so that you can watch it critically.

Think carefully about the order of your routines. You will want to begin and end with something quite spectacular, and during your act you will want some pauses, during which your audience can applaud and you can catch your breath. Keep to the order you have rehearsed so that you know exactly what you are going to do next and where your props are.

You must also decide if you are going to be silent throughout your act or if you are going to talk. If you decide to introduce the routines, take care to choose your moment carefully. If you announce the pattern too soon, the element of surprise is lost; if you leave it too late, your words may be drowned by the audience's reaction. If, for example, you include juggler's tennis in your routine, you may want to shout "Smash" or "Volley" as you rush from one side of the stage to the other. If you drop a ball, say "Love – 15."

Showmanship is just as important as skill. However skilled you are and however long and hard you have practiced the patterns and routines, you are still fallible, and even the most accomplished jugglers drop their props on occasion. You can sometimes cover for a dropped ball by making a joke of it to your audience, or you can make the cover-up part of the routine:

1 **Continue to juggle while you drop to your knees to recover the dropped prop.**

If it goes a long way astray, ask a member of the audience to toss it back to you (this requires considerable practice, because the returned prop is going to be coming at a different angle and/or speed, and you must be ready for it).

Drop all the other balls or clubs. Leave them on the floor while you do something else for a while.

Take a book with "How to Juggle" written on the cover in large letters from your back pocket.

Do another trick – for example, if you are juggling with three clubs and you drop one, go into a routine with two clubs.

Kick the fallen prop back up into your pattern.

Children are always fascinated by juggling, and they generally want to join in. You might introduce the idea of having a "difficult" ball, which should be a different color from the other ones you are using. You can simply juggle a basic cascade, but make this ball shoot out at odd angles. Make it look as if you are having trouble catching it. Let it fly out into the audience so that one of the children can throw it back to you. Juggle high – your audience will tend to watch the balls that are in the air – and take the opportunity to hide the "difficult" ball under your arm. Continue with the other balls, asking the children where the ball has gone, then distract their attention somehow (shout "It's over there") and bring the ball back into your routine.

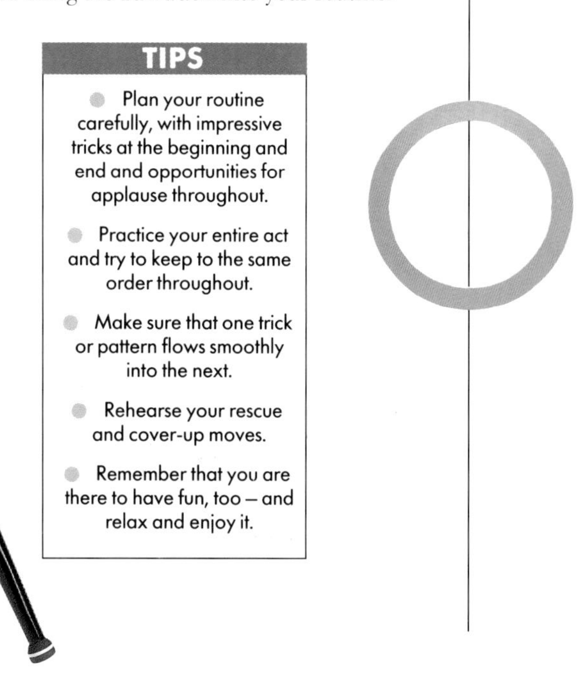

TIPS

- Plan your routine carefully, with impressive tricks at the beginning and end and opportunities for applause throughout.
- Practice your entire act and try to keep to the same order throughout.
- Make sure that one trick or pattern flows smoothly into the next.
- Rehearse your rescue and cover-up moves.
- Remember that you are there to have fun, too – and relax and enjoy it.